Over My De...

A comedy

Derek Benfield

Samuel French — London
New York - Toronto - Hollywood

CHARACTERS

Gerald James, a widower

Shirley Tyler, his daughter

Mark Tyler, his son-in-law

Amanda Eddison, his sister-in-law

Isobel French, an old friend

Carol Capstick, a cleaning lady

The action of the play takes place in the drawing-room of
Gerald's and Helen's house in the country

ACT I   Early evening on a Friday in late summer
ACT II   Later the same evening

Time — the present

Other plays by Derek Benfield
published by Samuel French Ltd

Anyone for Breakfast?
Bedside Manners
Beyond a Joke
A Bird in the Hand
Caught on the Hop
Don't Lose the Place!
Fish Out of Water
A Fly in the Ointment
Flying Feathers
Funny Business
In at the Deep End
In for the Kill
Look Who's Talking
Off the Hook!
Panic Stations
Post Horn Gallop
Running Riot
Second Time Around
Touch and Go
Two and Two Together
Up and Running
Wild Goose Chase

ACT I

The drawing-room of Helen's and Gerald's house in the country has three doors: one leading into the hall; one, on the opposite side, into the garden; and the third into the kitchen. The unseen dining-room (which plays an important part in the evening's events!) can be reached from both the hall and the kitchen. The furniture is tasteful antique: a desk below the hall door; a sofa centrally with a table behind it and a coffee table beside it; and an armchair with a table on which is a photograph of Helen. Below the garden door is a welcoming drinks table. Helen — now deceased — had good taste (if we are to assume that the taste is hers and not Gerald's) and the result is relaxing and welcoming. A pleasant place to live. And to die, for that matter ...

It is early evening on a Friday in late summer and the sun is shining

Nobody about. Then a head appears — rather furtively — around the door from the hall. The head belongs to Gerald, a pleasant, jovial man of 69. Seeing no sign of anyone he tiptoes across to the television set. He smiles mischievously, an ageing schoolboy, and turns the set on

Gerald is not alone, however. His daughter Shirley looks in from the hall, laden with shopping, and sees what he is up to

Shirley Didn't take *you* long!

Gerald jumps nervously, turns and sees her

Gerald What?
Shirley Mother's only been buried a week and already you're turning the television on.

Gerald turns the television off guiltily

Gerald I didn't hear you arrive.
Shirley Don't tell me you've become a secret telly watcher since the funeral?
Gerald I wanted to see the news.
Shirley They're hardly likely to mention it on that.
Gerald No. No, of course not! (*He laughs nervously*) It's old news now, anyway. Well — a week old.

Shirley puts down her shopping and runs to him emotionally and takes his hand

Shirley You always watched the television *together*! That's what I meant.
Gerald But your mother's not here anymore.
Shirley Exactly! And you can't watch it on your own.
Gerald Not *ever*?
Shirley Well … Not quite so soon — after …

Gerald thinks about this for a second

Gerald Why not?
Shirley (*sentimentally*) Because *she's* not watching it …
Gerald She might be for all we know. They probably have digital in heaven by now.
Shirley Anyway, what would the neighbours think? We only buried Mummy a week ago and already you're watching the television.
Gerald It was only the news. I wasn't watching *Heartbeat*.
Shirley (*sadly*) But don't you see? You were doing it on your *own*.
Gerald I haven't much choice, have I?
Shirley You're supposed to be grieving.
Gerald I *am* grieving. That doesn't mean I can't keep up with what's going on in the world.
Shirley Mummy would expect you to be grieving.
Gerald No, she wouldn't.
Shirley How do you know?

Gerald moves away, wondering how he would know. He thinks of something

Gerald She told me.
Shirley (*doubting this*) When?
Gerald What does it matter when? Did you bring the evening paper? (*He forages amongst her shopping*) Or am I banned from that, as well? (*He finds it*) Ah …
Shirley (*persisting*) When?
Gerald (*looking up from the evening paper; innocently*) What?
Shirley When did Mummy tell you that she wouldn't expect you to grieve?
Gerald Oh — (*lying*) three weeks ago.
Shirley Two weeks before she died?
Gerald At school you never used to be good at sums. What happened?
Shirley What day was it?
Gerald Can't remember.

Shirley She was making this important statement about the possible nature
of your grieving and you can't remember the day?
Gerald I *can* remember the day! Just not the name of the day.
Shirley (*going to him*) All right — what did she say, then?
Gerald (*hiding in the newspaper*) H'm? When?

Shirley takes the paper from him and casts it on to the sofa

Shirley Three weeks ago! On an apparently unmemorable day of the week.
Gerald It *was* memorable.
Shirley But you've forgotten?
Gerald No! It was memorable for what she said, not for the name of the day.
Shirley Go on, then! What did she say?

Gerald drifts away, avoiding her eyes

Gerald She said — and you may find this difficult to believe — she said that
if she went first … (*He hesitates, uncertainly*)
Shirley You make it sound as if she was going to Harrogate.
Gerald (*persevering*) If she pre-deceased me, she didn't want me to grieve.

Shirley thinks this rather out of character for her mother

Shirley Mother said that?
Gerald Yes. I told you.
Shirley She said you weren't to grieve?
Gerald Yes.
Shirley Not *ever*?
Gerald Well — not to excess.
Shirley And you think a week is excessive?
Gerald I'm only telling you what she said! (*He dives into Shirley's shopping
to escape*) You seem to have been doing a lot of shopping.
Shirley Yes. I'm going to cook you a lovely big dinner tonight.
Gerald (*not keen*) Ah …
Shirley Don't you like the idea?
Gerald I shall probably be busy grieving.
Shirley You can grieve and eat at the same time.
Gerald Well, I … I'm not very hungry. (*He sits on the sofa and rescues the
evening paper*)

*Shirley immediately becomes sad. She runs to Gerald sympathetically, sits
down and embraces him*

Shirley Of course you aren't! How could you be? I shouldn't have asked.

How can you be expected to eat at a time like this? I'm sorry, Daddy. I shouldn't have suggested it. It was thoughtless of me.

Gerald No, no! It's just that I had a double hamburger at lunchtime.

Shirley (*unable to believe her ears*) A double hamburger?

Gerald Yes. (*A beat*) With french fries and a green salad.

Shirley (*getting up in surprise*) Daddy! How could you?

Gerald Well, I was hungry *then*.

Shirley You were eating a double hamburger a week after Mummy's funeral? What will people think?

Gerald She told me to.

Shirley When?

Gerald hesitates briefly

Gerald Three weeks ago.

Shirley (*suspiciously*) On the same day that she talked about grieving?

Gerald Yes. It was a sort of double-whammy. She said whatever happened I must try to eat properly. And be *seen* to eat properly.

Shirley I don't believe you!

Gerald You can ask her. Oh, no — of course you can't, can you?

Shirley Mummy would never say a thing like that. Hamburgers in public after her funeral indeed!

Gerald Not immediately after. I didn't go straight there from the graveyard. If I'd known I was going to be cross-examined I'd have asked her to put it in writing.

Shirley (*looking critically at Gerald's sports jacket*) And I think that jacket's a bit lively a week after burying your wife.

Gerald (*glancing at his jacket*) Is it? Oh.

Shirley You haven't been on the links, have you?

Gerald Links?

Shirley Golf links! Isn't that what you call it?

Gerald (*realizing*) Oh. Yes. No, I haven't.

Shirley I'm very surprised.

Gerald That's not a very nice way to speak to a grieving widower.

Shirley But you're not an ordinary grieving widower, are you, Daddy?

Gerald What do you expect me to wear? Sackcloth and ashes? Anyway, I promised Helen not to wear dark colours.

Shirley (*giving him an old-fashioned look*) When?

Gerald (*guiltily*) H'm?

Shirley Three weeks ago?

Gerald (*gratefully*) Yes!

Shirley You must have been very surprised. All these requests — out of the blue — about your impending widowerhood when she wasn't expecting to die.

Gerald Of course she was expecting to die.

Shirley (*anxiously*) She told you that?

Gerald No. But we had both retired. And after retiring death's the only definite thing left on the agenda. (*He grins at her*)

Shirley (*giving him a push*) Oh, Daddy … ! Did Mummy make any *other* requests about your life as a widower? Join the local darts club? Something like that?

Gerald No — of course not!

Shirley I'm very surprised. She seems to have spent a lot of time compiling her list of post funeral promises.

Gerald (*defensively*) Well, *I* did the same!

Shirley looks at him, uncertain whether he is sending her up or not

Shirley You mean you gave Mummy a similar list of requests in case *you* went first?

Gerald Yes. We were having one of those conversations. You know how it is.

Shirley (*laughing*) No, I don't!

Gerald No, no! Of course you don't! Elderly conversations. Wanting-to-leave-everything-tidy conversations.

Shirley Like a pre-nuptial agreement?

Gerald Yes. Only this was a pre-probate agreement.

Shirley But how could you know which of your agreements was going to apply?

Gerald First past the post.

Shirley realizes that he is joking; they laugh

> *Mark comes in from the hall. He is in his forties and carries a laptop computer and a briefcase. He is surprised to find Shirley and Gerald laughing*

Mark (*anxiously*) Is something wrong?

Gerald No, no. Come on in. Everything's fine.

Mark I heard you laughing.

Gerald We'll try not to do it again.

Mark and Shirley kiss, briefly; a well-practised habit

Mark
Shirley } (*together*) Hallo, darling.

Mark puts down his things and moves to Gerald

Mark (*sombrely*) Hallo, Gerry ...

Gerald (*cheerfully, as if seeing Mark for the first time*) Hallo, Mark! Have a good day?

Mark is slightly taken aback by Gerald's bonhomie

Mark Sorry?

Gerald At the office. You have been at the office today, haven't you?

Mark Ah — yes — all day.

Gerald Good man. So *did* you?

Mark What?

Gerald Have a good day.

Mark Oh. Yes. Quite good. Did you? No — sorry — that's a silly question. Of course you didn't!

Gerald Wasn't a bad day, actually.

Mark (*surprised*) Really? Oh, great!

Gerald I walked around the pond.

Mark (*gazing at Gerald with infinite admiration*) Around the pond? Well done!

Gerald It wasn't very difficult.

Mark Well, *I* think it was bloody brave of you!

Gerald It's not peopled by crocodiles, you know. A few Canada geese, that's about all. And *they're* not too perilous.

Mark I meant ... under the circumstances.

Gerald I have done it before.

Mark What? Since — er ... ? (*He gestures, vaguely*)

Gerald (*amused by Mark's discomfort*) No. Not since — er ... (*He copies Mark's gesture*)

Embarrassed, Shirley hastily gathers up her bags of shopping

Shirley Well, I think I'll go into the kitchen.

Gerald (*indicating*) It's through there. You can't miss it. It's got a fridge and a cooker and a washing machine and things. Easily identifiable. As a kitchen.

Shirley Daddy, I know where it is. Mark and I have been living here for ten days.

Gerald Yes — of course you have. I'd forgotten.

Shirley (*to Mark*) I'm cooking a big dinner tonight!

Mark (*a little fearfully*) Are you? (*To Gerald*) Is she?

Gerald Apparently.

Mark Oh ...

Shirley (*to Mark, pointedly*) Anyway, you want to ... *talk*, don't you?

Mark Do I?
Shirley I'll see you later, then, Daddy.
Gerald I expect I'll still be here.

Shirley nods encouragingly at Mark, smiles at Gerald and goes into the kitchen with her shopping

Mark looks at Gerald, a little apprehensive

Mark A big dinner, eh?
Gerald Sounds like it. And she does seem to be heavily laden.
Mark H'm ... (*Suddenly*) Can I get you a drink?
Gerald (*getting up*) No, no! I'll do it. It is still my house. *(He chuckles, then stops in sudden doubt)* Isn't it?
Mark Yes, of course!
Gerald Oh, good. That is a relief. I was worried about probate, you see. Whisky?
Mark Thanks.
Gerald Water?
Mark No, thanks.

Gerald goes to see to the drinks. Mark sits down on the sofa and tries to relax, without success, crossing and uncrossing his legs

Er ... Er ... See anyone you know?
Gerald Where?
Mark Walking around the pond.
Gerald Oh. No. The local widows haven't started gathering yet.
Mark (*puzzled*) Sorry?
Gerald Never mind. It was meant to be a joke.
Mark (*realizing*) Oh — right. (*So he laughs*) Yes, of course! Widows, eh? Ha! Ha! Yes ... (*His laughter dies*)
Gerald (*arriving with their drinks*) Whisky.
Mark (*taking his drink*) Thanks.

Gerald sits down next to Mark

Gerald Nuts?
Mark (*jumping*) What?
Gerald Nuts? (*He offers the dish of nuts*)
Mark No, thanks. I'm not very good with nuts.
Gerald Really? Don't mind if *I* have some, do you? I mean, you don't object to nuts as such?

Mark No, no — you go ahead.
Gerald They don't bother me, you see. I can usually handle my nuts quite
  well.

*Gerald handles his nuts in silence for a moment. Neither of them has as yet
touched his whisky. Gerald realizes that Mark is probably waiting for the
starting gun, so he raises his glass*

  Well — here's to your mother-in-law!

*Mark is not good at relationships, and for a moment is unsure to whom
Gerald is referring*

Mark Who?
Gerald The one in the graveyard.
Mark (*realizing*) Oh — yes — sorry!
Gerald You never *were* good at relationships, were you?
Mark Well, you do have a big family.
Gerald It's smaller than it was.
Mark Ah. Yes. (*Raising his glass*) To my — er — —
Gerald Mother-in-law.
Mark Yes.

*They clink their glasses and sip their drinks. A bleak silence. Then Mark
suddenly activates himself*

Mark Good heavens! I almost forgot!
Gerald What?
Mark I've got something for you.

Gerald considers this

Gerald I hope it's not a cat.
Mark Sorry?
Gerald I've never had a cat, you see. And I'm not going to have one now
  even if my wife *is* dead.
Mark Oh — no! No — it's not a cat.
Gerald Good. That's all right then.

*Mark goes to his briefcase, takes out a small package, brings it to Gerald and
holds it out to him. Gerald stares at the package, puzzled*

  What is it?

Mark It's for you. A sort of present.

Gerald Not my birthday, is it? I don't think I'm up to two big occasions in one week.

Mark I thought you might like them.

Gerald You mean there's more than one of whatever it is?

Mark (*amused*) I should jolly well hope so!

Gerald (*taking the package*) Thanks. (*He waits for a moment, gazing at his present*) Shall I open it *now*?

Mark Unless you'd rather do it in your bedroom.

Gerald Is it something to use in the bedroom, then?

Mark No, no! I just thought you'd prefer to open it in secret.

Gerald You mean you don't want me to open it in here?

Mark Well, you can if you like …

Gerald Right. I will then. (*He is about to open the package*)

Mark She won't be back for a minute.

Gerald Who?

Mark My wife.

Gerald Shirley?

Mark (*amused*) Well, I haven't got another one. She's in the kitchen.

Gerald I know. She's seeing to the dinner.

Mark So you've plenty of time.

Gerald considers this for a moment

Gerald She's a slow cook, then, is she?

Mark Well — you know — she does need to consult a cookery book occasionally.

Gerald (*knowingly*) Ah — yes.

They laugh

Mark So you should have plenty of time.

Gerald It won't take me very long to open this package.

Mark I didn't mean that.

Gerald Doesn't Shirley like to see people opening packages?

Mark Well — that depends what's in it, doesn't it?

Gerald I see. (*He thinks about this*) What *is* in it?

Mark I can't tell you that! It's a surprise!

Gerald It certainly is! A surprise *and* a secret, apparently. A secret from Shirley, that is.

Mark Well — she doesn't know about it, yes.

Gerald And you don't *want* her to know about it?

Mark It might be better.

Gerald For her not to know about it?

Mark Yes. She might take it as an insult.

Gerald Oh, dear. I'd better open it, then. And if you hear Shirley coming back give me the nod and I'll hide whatever it is under the sofa.

Mark Right! (*He smiles conspiratorially*)

Gerald Here we go, then.

Gerald starts to open the package — very carefully. Mark notices his caution

Mark It's all right. It won't explode.

Gerald That *is* a relief. I don't want to join Helen just yet!

Gerald opens the package to reveal a few dainty sandwiches. He picks one up and looks at it, puzzled naturally

Sandwiches?

Mark Yes. (*A beat*) Smoked salmon.

Gerald Smoked salmon sandwiches?

Mark Yes. On brown.

Gerald Oh. Right ... (*He stares at the sandwiches*)

Mark (*in sudden panic*) You do *like* smoked salmon, don't you?

Gerald Oh, yes. Yes. Especially on brown.

Mark Good! I was sure you would.

Gerald You were right. My favourite.

Mark I thought it would be a nice surprise.

Gerald It is! And it's the first time.

Mark Sorry?

Gerald Nobody's ever given me a present of smoked salmon sandwiches before.

Mark Really?

Gerald Not that I can remember, anyway. It's quite a new departure.

Mark (*pleased*) I did the right thing, then?

Gerald You certainly did.

Mark Great.

A pause. Gerald considers, gazing at the sandwiches. Mark waits for a moment

(*Anxiously*) Well, go on! Don't hang about!

Gerald You mean I've got to eat them *now*?

Mark That was the idea. I thought you'd be dying for them. Sorry! I didn't mean to say dying. Longing! Longing for them. I thought you'd be a bit peckish left on your own all day. Sorry! I didn't mean to say left on your own!

Gerald That's all right, Mark. And please don't think I'm not grateful, because I am. It was a very nice thought. Very nice indeed. Fancy you — busy at your lap-top — suddenly thinking, "I'll take the old man some smoked salmon sandwiches — on brown — because that's what he'll be dying for — longing for!" It's just that I ... I can't understand why.

Mark (*puzzled*) Why?

Gerald Yes.

Mark You said you *liked* smoked salmon sandwiches.

Gerald Yes. I do.

Mark So why do you ask why?

Gerald Because I don't understand ... *why* you did it.

Mark Ah.

Gerald You see? It is unusual.

Mark Ah. Yes. (*With difficulty*) Well ... You see — poor old Shirley ...

Gerald (*puzzled*) Sorry?

Mark She means well. In the kitchen department. But — (*he glances around to make sure she is not returning*) let's face it, Gerry, she's a pretty poor cook.

Gerald Well, I didn't like to ...

Mark But she *is*!

Gerald Yes, I know, but — —

Mark So I thought — after ten days of Shirley's cooking — you might be glad of something you really like.

Gerald (*realizing*) Ah! That's what you meant about not insulting her? You didn't want Shirley to know about the — er ...

Mark Smoked salmon sandwiches.

Gerald Yes.

Mark Exactly!

Gerald That's all right. It can be our little secret.

Mark Great!

Gerald It was very considerate of you, Mark, and I do appreciate it.

Mark (*anxiously*) Get on with them, then!

Gerald Oh — right. (*He takes a sandwich and starts to eat it, slowly*)

Mark watches him hopefully

Mark OK?

Gerald H'm. Very nice. Very nice indeed. Better than the rissoles last night, eh?

Mark Yes — rather!

They laugh together. Gerald does not embark on a second sandwich

What's the matter?

Gerald Nothing. They're very nice. But I … I'm not very hungry.

Mark suddenly realizes how difficult it must be to eat when you have just lost your wife, and sits beside Gerald sympathetically

Mark Oh, God! Of course you're not! I should have realized. I'm so sorry, Gerry. It's bound to affect your appetite, losing your wife like that.
Gerald (*modestly*) Well, yes, it's not as if she was just trying to find her way out of Tesco's, is it?
Mark No. Bound to put you off your food a bit. (*He starts to eat a sandwich himself*) H'm. These are rather good.
Gerald It wasn't that, though.
Mark (*eating*) H'm? Not the fact of your wife dying? Sorry! I didn't mean to say dying — —
Gerald Well, not *just* that.
Mark Then what?
Gerald (*a little ashamed*) Well, at lunchtime I … I had a double hamburger in the pub near the pond.

Mark stares at him in disbelief, finishing off his sandwich

Mark You *didn't*?
Gerald Yes.
Mark A double hamburger?
Gerald H'm.
Mark In the pub?
Gerald Yes. (*A beat*) With french fries and a green salad.

Mark gazes at him in admiration, and pats him on the back

Mark Good man! I really admire you, Gerry. You're putting on a brave front. I knew you would. Life has to go on. You don't mind me eating these, do you? I didn't get any lunch.
Gerald Please. Be my guest.

Mark helps himself to another sandwich

The door opens, heralding Shirley's return from the kitchen

Gerald hastily shoves the packet of sandwiches under the sofa and Mark quickly finishes his sandwich, so they look suitably composed when Shirley arrives and looks at them confidently

Shirley Everything's under control.
Mark (*surprised*) Is it?
Shirley Yes! (*Then losing heart*) I think so …
Mark (*hopefully*) It'll take some time, though, won't it?
Shirley Well, yes. It's got to be cooked, hasn't it?
Mark (*to Gerald, aside*) That'll make a change … !
Shirley Did you get everything sorted out, then?
Mark Er — yes. We got everything sorted out, didn't we, Gerry?
Gerald Certainly did!

Shirley looks at them suspiciously for a moment

Shirley You're both looking very furtive.
Gerald ⎫
Mark ⎬ (*together*) No, we're not!
Shirley I hope you're not hiding something from me?
Gerald ⎫
Mark ⎬ (*together*) No! Never!
Gerald We were having a drink, that's all.
Mark And we never look furtive when we're having a drink.
Shirley Yes, you do!
Gerald Well, *you'd* better have one, then you won't notice. (*Getting up*) What'll it be?
Shirley Oh — sherry, please.
Gerald One sherry coming up. (*He goes to pour a sherry*)

Shirley turns to Mark and mouths silently, "Did you ask him?" Mark pretends not to know what she is saying

Gerald returns with a glass of sherry and notices Shirley mouthing at Mark

  Sherry, Shirley!

Shirley hastily covers up and accepts her sherry

Shirley Thanks, Daddy. (*She sits down in the armchair and sips her sherry, then looks at Gerald; hopefully*) So what do you think of the arrangement, then?
Gerald (*blankly*) H'm? What arrangement?
Shirley (*glaring at Mark*) I thought you two had been talking!
Mark We were! We did! We have!
Shirley Good! (*To Gerald*) So what do you think of it?
Gerald Think of what?

Shirley (*glaring at Mark again*) You said you'd been talking!

Mark Yes, but not about that. (*Profoundly*) Your father went for a walk. That's good news, isn't it?

Shirley (*patiently*) I *know* he went for a walk.

Mark Around the pond.

Shirley Yes! He told me!

Gerald Twice, actually.

Shirley What?

Gerald I walked around the pond twice. (*Gesturing*) Once that way, and once that way.

Shirley You must have worked up quite an appetite, then?

Gerald $\Big\}$ (*together*) No!
Mark

Shirley Well, I shall be very disappointed if you don't do justice to my cooking. I've made an extra effort tonight.

Mark Oh. Good ... (*He exchanges a look with Gerald*)

Shirley And as a special treat we're going to have smoked salmon for starters.

Another look between the men

Mark Smoked salmon?

Shirley Yes.

Gerald With brown bread?

Shirley (*puzzled*) If you like.

Gerald Well, that's what you usually have with smoked salmon. Isn't it, Mark?

Mark Yes — it certainly is! (*He tries to conceal his amusement*)

Shirley You do *like* smoked salmon, don't you?

Gerald Oh, yes — we like smoked salmon, don't we, Mark?

Mark Yes! Especially with brown bread.

Shirley Oh, good!

Gerald So — what arrangement were you talking about?

Shirley Sorry?

Gerald You asked what I thought of the arrangement.

Shirley Ah — yes. (*To Mark; hopefully*) Darling ...

Mark (*innocently*) What?

Gerald (*to Mark*) Was there something you were supposed to talk to me about?

Mark (*blankly*) No — I don't think so ...

Shirley Yes, there was! (*To Gerald*) He was supposed to tell you about the plans we've made!

Gerald (*smiling; delightedly*) You're going to India! Oh, good! You've always talked about going there, but I never thought you'd do it. I *am* impressed.

Shirley No, we're not!

Gerald *Not* going to India?

Shirley No.

Gerald Littlehampton?

Shirley We're not going anywhere!

Gerald Oh, dear. What a pity. What plans were you talking about, then?

Shirley Plans for *you*, of course!

Gerald For *me*? I didn't think I'd got any plans. Not now that Helen's gone. Not yet, anyhow. (*He sips his whisky*)

Shirley (*desperately*) Daddy — you can't stay in this house!

Gerald It's not subsiding, is it?

Shirley (*appealing to Mark helplessly*) Mark — —?

Mark, who was enjoying his whisky, tries to be helpful

Mark Shirley's right. You can't stay here on your own.

Gerald But I live here.

Mark Yes — yes, I know you live here, Gerry — —

Gerald Helen and I were married here, and this is our home. The place where we live.

Mark (*wildly*) That's why you can't stay here! You wouldn't like it here now that Helen's dead. Sorry! I didn't mean to say dead!

Gerald (*surprised by this sudden outburst*) What are you suggesting, then?

Shirley and Mark exchange a look. This is it. They've got to do it now. Shirley plucks up courage and says it

Shirley We want you to move in with *us*.

A brief silence as Gerald considers this

Gerald With you?

Shirley With Mark and me and the boys.

There is another brief silence. Then Gerald laughs!

Gerald You're joking, aren't you?

Shirley Of course we're not joking! We'd *like* you to live with us. Wouldn't we, Mark?

Mark (*looking up from his whisky*) Yes — of course we would!

Gerald Well, *I* wouldn't.

They stare at him in surprise

Shirley Daddy! Why not?

Gerald is uncertain for a moment. Then he invents an escape route

Gerald Well, for one thing — you never make lists.
Shirley Lists?
Gerald Yes …
Shirley What sort of lists?
Gerald Housekeeping lists. What things are running out. Flour. Sugar. That sort of thing. When the Council Tax is due. Your mother was a great list-maker. It was something you never learned from her. I could never live in a house without lists. (*He suffers at the thought*)
Shirley (*helpfully*) Well … I could start making lists.
Gerald No! No — you'd never keep it up! If you haven't made lists by your age it's too late to start.
Shirley (*in disbelief*) And that's all that's stopping you coming to live with us?

Gerald thinks perhaps he needs to consolidate

Gerald Well — it's not *just* that.
Shirley Not just lists?
Gerald No.
Shirley What else, then?
Gerald Well — er — (*turning to Mark*) you haven't started oiling your garden tools by any chance, have you?
Mark (*bewildered*) Sorry?
Gerald Spade. Fork. Mowing-machine — that kind of thing?
Mark Ah — no — I'm afraid that's one of my blind spots.
Gerald (*grinning triumphantly*) Exactly! And that would always worry me. If I was a permanent guest at your place … I'd go into the garden shed — wanting to help with a little light digging — and I'd find the fork all covered in rust. You really should take care of your equipment, you know. I always oil *my* equipment.
Mark You could oil mine *for* me.
Gerald No, no, I couldn't do that! A man has to take care of his own tools.
Shirley So you don't want to come and live with us just because I don't make lists and Mark doesn't oil his tools?

Gerald realizes that he must make a more personal approach

Gerald You wouldn't like me living with you. I'd drive you mad in no time. I'd be in the way. The boys would hate it.

Shirley No, they wouldn't!

Gerald Grandfathers should be taken out and dusted at Christmas and on birthdays. The rest of the year they should be packed away in a cardboard box.

Mark You get on well with the boys. You can talk sport to them. They'd like that. You know all about football and cricket. And you always watch the Ryder Cup.

Shirley Yes! They'd love it!

Gerald (*quietly*) It's not *them* I'm thinking about …

Shirley (*dramatically*) But you're my father! And you're all alone! And I want you to live with me and my family!

Gerald and Mark do not react to Shirley's dramatics, obviously quite used to them

Gerald Well, that's very sweet of you, Shirley, and I do appreciate it. But I'm afraid it's a non-starter. You see, *this* is my home — Helen's and mine — and we want to go on living here.

Shirley (*emotionally*) But *she's* not here any more!

Gerald Yes, she is. Of course she is. She's over here. (*He picks up the framed photograph of Helen*)

Shirley Daddy, that's just a photograph!

Gerald Yes. But *she's* here as well. Not just in a photograph. She's everywhere. In every room. She'll always be here. (*He puts down the photograph*) I can talk to her while I'm doing the dusting.

Mark If you start wandering about the house talking to pictures they'll take you away in a plain van!

Gerald (*with a grin*) That'll solve the problem, then, won't it?

The front doorbell rings imperiously

Shirley You're not expecting anyone, are you?

Gerald No. But life's full of surprises.

Shirley Perhaps it's the vicar.

Mark You're not expecting the vicar, surely?

Gerald Certainly not! I saw him last week.

Mark (*intrigued*) Did you really?

Gerald You remember! He was at Helen's funeral.

Mark looks blank

He was the one who was dressed up and did all the talking.

Shirley (*gently remonstrating*) Daddy ... !
Gerald You'd better let him in.

Shirley puts down her glass and goes out into the hall

Mark is deep in thought

Mark I didn't know you'd ever *been* in my shed.
Gerald (*at a loss*) Sorry?
Mark My garden shed. When you noticed that I hadn't oiled my tools.
Gerald (*realizing*) Oh. Well, it — it was Easter Monday, I think. Yes, that was it! I'd gone to get out the croquet stuff.
Mark I don't remember that.
Gerald Oh, yes. Very sunny it was.
Mark I must have been away.

Shirley returns, rather uncertainly

Gerald *Is* it the vicar?
Shirley No. Worse.
Gerald Worse than the vicar, eh?
Shirley Aunt Amanda.
Gerald (*surprised*) My sister-in-law?
Shirley Yes.
Gerald That *is* worse than the vicar ... !

Amanda comes in from the hall. She is a confident, enthusiastic woman in her sixties. She is dressed in a smart, dark suit and carries a bunch of lilies

The others all look at her in surprise

Amanda Gerry!

Amanda abruptly passes her flowers to Shirley and crosses down to Gerald. She stares at him for a moment, heavy with sympathy

Oh, Gerry! I'm *so* sorry ... (*She engulfs Gerald in her arms*)

Gerald suffers bravely. Finally, Amanda releases him

Gerald There's no need to apologize.
Amanda (*a little put out*) I wasn't apologizing, Gerry. I was expressing sympathy.

Gerald Oh. Yes. Right. Thank you.
Amanda (*puzzled*) Why should I be apologizing? I'm not late, am I?

Gerald and Shirley exchange a look

Gerald Just a bit, yes.
Amanda The funeral is *tomorrow*, isn't it?
Gerald No. *Last* Saturday.

Amanda gazes at him, appalled

Amanda *Last* Saturday?
Gerald Yes.
Amanda But I was in Tanzania. I couldn't possibly have been here last Saturday.
Gerald Well, I'm sorry, but that's when it was.
Amanda Are you sure?
Gerald Yes. Definitely last Saturday.
Amanda Well, why didn't you wait for me?
Gerald We'd already booked the vicar.
Amanda Oh, dear … ! (*Remembering*) And I went and bought flowers! Lilies, too!
Gerald Very appropriate …
Shirley They're lovely. Must have cost you a fortune.
Amanda Yes, they did. (*Without enthusiasm*) Well, I suppose *you'd* better have them, then, Shirley.
Shirley No! No — I couldn't! (*She thrusts the flowers back into Amanda's hands*) They were for Mummy.
Amanda Well, they're no good to *her* now! (*She looks around for somewhere to put the flowers and sees Mark for the first time*) Oh, hallo, Mark … (*She embraces him, sadly but briefly*) I'm *so* sorry to see you.
Mark What?
Amanda On such a sad occasion. (*Confidentially*) Was it *really* last week?
Mark I'm afraid so.
Amanda I don't understand it. Helen *knew* I was going to Tanzania. Mind you, I did wonder when I saw that Gerry was dressed for the links. (*She looks disapprovingly at Gerald's jacket. To Mark*) Go and put these in water, there's a good boy. We don't want them to wilt, do we?
Mark No. Not when you've paid so much for them.

Mark takes the lilies from Amanda and goes out into the kitchen

Amanda gives Mark a critical look as he goes

Amanda (*turning to Shirley*) I always knew he had a sense of humour. (*She goes back to Gerald*) Oh, Gerry — I really am sorry for being late. What *would* Helen have thought?

Gerald I don't expect she'd have been surprised …

Amanda Gerry! That's very unfair.

Gerald Well, you always were forgetful.

Amanda But my own sister's funeral! And I should have been here to look after *you*.

Gerald That's all right. Shirley and Mark have been staying with me.

Amanda (*not too impressed*) Oh. Well, I'm sure they must have been a great comfort. (*She looks at the framed photograph of Helen*) Oh, that's such a *lovely* picture of Helen …

Gerald Yes.

Amanda She was the perfect sister to me, you know. And wife to you, too, of course! You poor man — you must miss her dreadfully. (*She notices his drink*) Still, you are drinking whisky. That's a good sign.

Gerald (*taking the hint*) Perhaps I can get *you* one, Amanda?

Amanda Oh, what a good idea! It's been a long day and I'm quite exhausted. (*She sits down on the sofa, exhausted*)

Gerald (*on his way to the drinks table*) Water?

Amanda Don't be silly, Gerry.

Gerald (*catching Shirley's eye*) One whisky, no water coming up. (*He starts to pour*)

Amanda (*suddenly activating herself*) I say! I've got a wonderful idea! I'm so mortified by getting the date of my sister's funeral wrong that I'm going to make it up to you all. (*With great effect*) I'm going to take you all out to dinner tonight. Champagne! The lot. We'll have a proper celebration!

Shirley It was a funeral, Aunt Amanda, not a wedding.

Gerald grins as he returns with a whisky

Amanda A celebration of her *life*. That's what I meant. (*Accepting the whisky*) Oh, thank you, Gerry. (*Raising her glass*) Well, here's to — er — —

Gerald No, no! We've done all that.

Amanda Sorry?

Gerald "Helen", "Mummy", "Mother-in-law" — we've done the lot.

Shirley How about "late sister"?

Gerald tries to stifle a laugh

Amanda (*giving Shirley a stern look*) Don't be flippant, Shirley. It doesn't suit you. (*So she abandons her toast and just sips her whisky*) This isn't the whisky you usually have.

Gerald No.

Amanda You usually have malt.

Gerald Yes. But I'm cutting down now that I'm a widower.

Amanda (*looking at her whisky disapprovingly*) I wondered why you offered me water. So — dinner tonight, then?

Gerald and Shirley exchange a look

Gerald Well — actually — Shirley's already arranged to cook dinner.

Amanda (*looking doubtfully at Shirley*) She hasn't, has she?

Shirley Yes. I'm making a special effort.

Amanda Oh, dear …

Mark returns with the lilies resplendent in a vase

Mark There we are! How's that? (*He sets the lilies down*)

Shirley Oh, lovely! Well done, darling! They look beautiful.

Amanda So they should. Honestly, the price you pay for flowers these days. Mind you, they look much better *here*. I always think flowers at funerals are such a waste, don't you? Just left there lying in the rain. It's rather sad, really.

Shirley I think they go to hospitals.

Amanda (*unimpressed*) Oh. Do they? Well, I suppose that's all right. (*Turning to Mark*) I was thinking of taking you all out to dinner tonight, Mark.

Mark (*enthusiastically*) Oh, good! What a great idea! I'm starving! Aren't you, darling? (*He sees Shirley's stony look and his enthusiasm dies*) Ah …

Amanda But apparently Shirley's got it under control.

Mark Has she? Have you? I mean, it's … It's under way, is it? It can't be — well — you know — put off — can it? Till tomorrow? Put off till … No? Right. Sorry. I'd forgotten. Nice idea, though. Wasn't it, Gerry? No? Right.

Amanda We'll have to do it another night.

Gerald *Another* night?

Mark What a good idea! (*Moving to Gerald*) Mind you, it'll have to be quick, won't it, Gerry? (*He grins at him*)

Gerald Will it?

Mark Of course it will!

Shirley (*puzzled*) Oh. I didn't know that.

Mark (*teasing him*) You never told us, did you? You old dog! (*To the others*) He never told us, did he?

Shirley and Amanda silently shake their heads in puzzled unison

Your father's a dark horse, Shirley.

Gerald An old dog *and* a dark horse?

Amanda What are you talking about, Mark?

Mark And for what it's worth, Gerry — I think you're making the correct decision. You've got the right attitude! I knew you would have. The moment you told me about walking around the pond. I knew you were on the right track. No sense in mooning about in here all on your own. Life has to go on! So — tell us — we're all dying to know — sorry! I didn't mean to say dying! Longing! Longing to know!

Gerald Longing to know what?

Mark (*playfully*) Which direction are you heading in, old sea dog?

Gerald (*to Shirley*) I'm an old sea dog now ...

Mark Are the Seychelles on your agenda?

Gerald The Seychelles? Good lord, no.

Mark Something more modest, perhaps? (*A terrible thought*) Oh, no! Not the Canaries with SAGA? You wouldn't like that. They're all *old* people.

Gerald I'm not going anywhere!

Mark (*appalled*) You're not?

Gerald No. Whatever gave you that idea?

Mark I saw two suitcases in the hall.

Gerald Well, they're not mine!

Amanda No — they're mine!

The others look at her in horror

Gerald ⎫
          ⎬ (*together*) Yours?
Mark ⎭

Amanda Yes. Of course.

Gerald and Mark exchange an apprehensive look

Gerald (*trying to be optimistic*) Ah! You're on your way to the airport!

Amanda (*patiently*) No, Gerry. I've just come *from* the airport.

Gerald Yes. But tomorrow you're off again! Is that it? An overnight stop, then off on another of your trips? I know you're an inveterate traveller.

Amanda Oh, no. I've done enough travelling for a while, and now I'm going to settle down.

Gerald Then why have you brought two suitcases *here*?

Amanda Because I'm coming to stay, of course.

Gerald To stay?

Amanda Yes.

Gerald *Here*?

Amanda Yes.

Gerald Why?

Amanda (*as if to a child*) Because this is where you live, Gerry.

Gerald Yes, I know that, but — —

Mark (*helpfully*) I think she means she's staying tonight and going tomorrow. (*He looks at Amanda*)

Amanda No, she doesn't mean that.

Mark Doesn't she?

Amanda Certainly not!

Gerald (*optimistically*) Monday? You're staying for the weekend and going home on Monday?

Amanda Don't be silly, Gerry. If I was only coming for the weekend I wouldn't have brought two suitcases, would I?

Gerald I know! Oxfam! You and Helen always supported the Third World. So you've brought two suitcases to pack up Helen's clothes and take them all to Oxfam.

Amanda (*a little shocked*) Gerry! I think that would be a little premature.

Shirley Yes, Daddy — it certainly would!

Gerald Oh. Right. (*To Amanda*) So why *have* you brought two suitcases, then?

Amanda Because I promised Helen.

Gerald Promised Helen you'd give me your old suitcases?

Amanda They are not old suitcases! I wouldn't be seen dead with old suitcases.

Mark Sorry! She didn't mean to say dead!

Amanda I made a solemn promise to Helen that if anything happened to her I'd look after you. We were having coffee in Selfridges. I remember it quite clearly.

Shirley You mean you were having one of those "elderly" conversations? One of those "wanting-to-leave-everything-tidy" conversations?

Amanda However did you guess?

Shirley A geriatric I know told me all about it. (*She grins at Gerald*)

Mark You promised Helen that you'd look after Gerry?

Amanda Yes. A solemn promise. And a promise I intend to keep.

Gerald tries to re-group his forces, and moves to Amanda

Gerald Ah — now — er … Now look, Amanda — I think you must have misunderstood. An easy thing to do over coffee. Especially in Selfridges. Helen probably meant that you should stay for just a few days. And Mark and Shirley have been doing that, so it does look as if you've had a wasted journey. (*He grins optimistically*)

Amanda No, Gerry.

Gerald No?

Amanda No. Not just for a few days. For the rest of your life.

They all react, appalled at this prospect

Gerald The rest of my life?

Amanda I don't believe in half measures, Gerry. In fact I've already put my house on the market.

Gerald (*to Mark, aside*) I may as well join Helen *now*! And it would make it easier for the gravediggers. The earth would still be quite loose.

Mark (*quietly*) I'll get you another whisky.

Gerald (*quietly*) Good idea ... !

Mark hastens away to refill Gerald's glass

(*Persevering with Amanda*) Don't *I* have any say in the matter?

Amanda No, of course not. Helen and I knew you wouldn't be in a fit state to make decisions. So we made this one for you. Gerry — I'm trying to help.

Gerald Yes — yes, I know — and I don't want to appear ungrateful, but I'd really rather be here on my own.

Amanda You may think that, Gerry. You may even believe that. But under the stress of what's happened you're not in a position to know what's good for you.

Gerald I *do* know what's good for me!

Mark (*arriving with Gerald's whisky*) Whisky!

Gerald Exactly! (*He takes it and sips some, gratefully*)

Amanda You see, Gerry dear, at the moment you're not thinking straight — that's only natural — but you'll soon get used to the idea.

Gerald I don't *want* to get used to the idea! (*Then he thinks of a way out*) Anyway, I'm afraid it's out of the question!

Amanda Why?

Gerald (*after a quick glance at Shirley*) Because I've already agreed to go and live with Shirley and Mark.

Shirley and Mark react with some surprise

Amanda (*dismissing the idea*)What on earth for?

Gerald Because they asked me. Before you arrived. Didn't you, Shirley?

Shirley (*dutifully*) Y-yes! We certainly did!

Amanda And what did you say?

Gerald I said yes, of course! Didn't I, Mark?

Mark Y-yes ... ! (*He grins at Shirley*)

Mark and Shirley are enjoying Gerald's sudden about-face

Amanda (*in disbelief*) Why on earth did you say that?

Gerald Because I *want* to go and stay with Shirley. (*He emulates Shirley's earlier dramatics*) She's my daughter! And I'm all alone! And I want to go and live with my daughter and her family!

Amanda (*not impressed by his histrionics*) Don't be ridiculous! You'd be in the way. They've got two young boys. They don't want their grandfather plodding about all over the place.

Gerald Yes, they do! I get on very well with the boys. Don't I, Mark?

Mark Yes — definitely!

Shirley You can talk sport to them, can't you, Daddy?

Gerald Yes! I know all about cricket!

Mark (*helpfully*) And football!

Gerald Yes — definitely football!

Mark (*nodding; encouragingly*) And you always watch the Ryder Cup.

Gerald Yes — every year!

Mark (*correcting him; quietly*) Every *two* years … !

Gerald So that's that, I'm afraid, Amanda. I'm moving in with them tomorrow. It's all arranged.

Amanda But that was before you knew *I* was coming, wasn't it?

Gerald (*chuckling; confidently*) Well, yes! But I promised, you see? And you can't go back on a promise, can you?

Amanda Nonsense. Of course you can! You won't be on your own now I'm here, so you can cancel the arrangement. I'm sure they'll understand.

Mark No, we won't!

Shirley And we've told the boys he's coming now!

Gerald (*surprised*) Have you? Oh, good! (*To Amanda*) So there we are. I'm going to live with Shirley and Mark, and that's that.

Amanda Don't be silly, Gerry. It wouldn't work. I know what you're like. Helen told me all about you.

Gerald *All* about me over a cup of coffee?

Amanda For one thing she said you're a man who likes lists.

Gerald reacts to this

(*Seeing his reaction*) There! She was right, wasn't she? You're an obsessive list-maker. I knew it! (*Looking disparagingly at Shirley*) And I bet Shirley's never made a list in her life!

Shirley I — I wouldn't mind starting …

Amanda Yes, you would. It's out of the question. (*To Gerald*) You're staying here with me, Gerry, and that's that. (*To Mark*) Be a dear and carry my suitcases upstairs, will you?

Mark looks uncertainly at Gerald. Gerald sighs, a defeated man, and shrugs helplessly

Mark starts to go

Amanda looks at Gerald and smiles, reassuringly

You'll be much better off with me, Gerry.

Gerald (*unconvinced*) Will I?

Amanda We'll be able to have long conversations sitting in front of the fire and sipping malt whisky.

Gerald There isn't any malt.

Amanda There is *now*! I brought some with me. (*She follows Mark, calling after him*) Mark! Mark — please be careful with my suitcases! They cost me a fortune!

Amanda disappears into the hall

Gerald sits down gloomily on the sofa. Shirley goes to him

Shirley Well — *what* a surprise … !

Gerald Yes. I'd sooner it had been the vicar.

Shirley You're not going to *let* her stay, are you?

Gerald I don't seem to have much choice …

Shirley Do you think Mummy *really* made Amanda promise to look after you?

Gerald Wouldn't be surprised. You know what your mother was like. Always a great one for forward planning.

Shirley (*reluctantly*) Well … I suppose I'll have to show Amanda where everything is, then?

Gerald Yes. I suppose so …

Shirley starts to go, then hesitates and looks back at the forlorn figure sitting on the sofa

Shirley Never mind, Daddy. Perhaps it's all for the best.

Gerald Whatever makes you think that?

Shirley smiles and goes out into the hall, closing the door behind her

Gerald sips his whisky, gloomily

Isobel appears outside in the garden. She was obviously once very pretty, and though now in her mid-sixties is still attractive and vivacious. She looks in from the garden and sees Gerald

Isobel Gerry!

Gerald jumps, surprised by the unexpected voice, and looks at Isobel without recognition

Gerald Can I help you? Are you looking for someone?
Isobel (*with a big smile*) Not any longer. (*She comes further into the room*)

Now getting a better look at her, Gerald realizes who she is and gets up in surprise

Gerald Good heavens! It's you!
Isobel Yes.
Gerald (*going to her*) Isobel! How nice to see you.
Isobel You took a long time to recognize me. It wasn't very flattering. Have I grown so old and ugly?
Gerald No! Never! I'm just not used to people entering from the garden. Not unless they're wearing boots. You took me by surprise.
Isobel (*sympathetically*) I'm so sorry …
Gerald Don't apologize. I'm delighted to see you.
Isobel I meant — about Helen.
Gerald Oh. Yes. Thank you. You heard, then?
Isobel I read about it in the paper. I was very sad for you.
Gerald Thanks. I should have let you know. I meant to, but — —
Isobel Don't worry. I understood.
Gerald I didn't think you lived around here any more.
Isobel I don't. I just thought I'd drive over and see if there was anything I could do to help.
Gerald You haven't brought two suitcases, have you?
Isobel Good heavens, no! Why should I do that?
Gerald Never mind. (*He smiles*) Come here! It's good to see you.

They embrace, fondly

Sit you down. Let me get you a drink. (*He goes to the drinks table*)
Isobel Thank you. (*She sits on the sofa*)
Gerald Gin and tonic?
Isobel Please.

Gerald sees to her drink

Gerald You haven't changed a bit.
Isobel It's too late to say that *now*!

They laugh

Gerald It must be years since Helen and I saw you.
Isobel Yes.
Gerald Time races by at our age, doesn't it? Nowadays, I find a week only
lasts three days. (*He takes Isobel her drink*)
Isobel (*accepting it*) Thanks. Cheers. (*She takes a sip, then looks up at him*)
I would have come to the funeral. If I'd known.

Gerald holds her look for a moment

Gerald Yes. I'm sorry.
Isobel How was it?
Gerald The flowers were lovely, the vicar was awful. It was quite obvious
that he'd never met her.
Isobel (*with a smile*) Well, they can't be expected to know all their
parishioners personally.
Gerald No. No, of course not! But I did give him Helen's CV and a couple
of family anecdotes, so he should have been able to make a bit more of a
job of it.
Isobel What did he say, then?
Gerald He told the congregation that Helen was very big in local affairs and
always gave a helping hand to the Boy Scouts. It made her sound like an
overweight paedophile. Still, Shirley and I would only have wept if he'd
done it too well, so at least he saved us from that embarrassment.
Isobel You're *supposed* to cry at funerals. It's part of the healing process.
Gerald Yes … (*He sits beside her*)

A sad pause

Isobel How is Shirley?
Gerald Oh, she's fine! A tower of strength. She and her husband have been
staying with me since Helen died.
Isobel I needn't have worried, then. You are being looked after.
Gerald Yes. But I'm glad to see you. You need old friends at a time like this.

They hold a sad look for the briefest of moments

How about you? You still married?
Isobel To which one?
Gerald Don't tell me you've had more than one since you divorced Alan?
Isobel Two at the last count.
Gerald And are you still married to either of them?
Isobel I'm afraid not.
Gerald What happened?

Isobel I gave them both the elbow.
Gerald I'm sorry. I didn't know. You always put "From us both" on your Christmas cards.
Isobel (*with a smile*) Well, that covers any eventuality, doesn't it?
Gerald What went wrong?
Isobel They didn't live up to expectations.
Gerald In what department?
Isobel *Every* department!

They laugh

Gerald Perhaps you set your targets too high.
Isobel Maybe I'd been spoilt.
Gerald (*holding her look*) Yes. Probably …

A brief pause, full of the past. Then she grins, breaking the moment

Isobel So now I'm a free woman again.
Gerald No toy-boy on the horizon?
Isobel Not yet. But I'm keeping my eyes open.

They laugh again, enjoying each other's company

   Where's Shirley hiding herself? Is she closeted in the kitchen?
Gerald No, no, she's upstairs with … (*He remembers who is upstairs and gets up, anxiously*) Oh, good heavens! For a moment I'd forgotten all about her … !
Isobel Forgotten all about who?

Mark comes in from the hall and sees Isobel

Mark Oh. Sorry. I didn't know we had company. I never heard the doorbell.
Isobel I didn't ring the doorbell. I came in from the garden.
Mark (*a little puzzled*) Oh. Right … (*He looks at Gerald, anticipating an introduction*) Er — Gerry … ?

But Gerald remains silent, his mind elsewhere

Isobel (*helpfully*) I'm an old friend.
Mark (*with a grin*) And old friends always come in from the garden?
Isobel I spotted Gerry through the window.
Mark (*intrigued*) Really? (*Turning to him*) Gerry — aren't you going to — er …?

Gerald (*his mind elsewhere*) Ah — yes — sorry. This is Mark. Shirley's
husband.

Isobel Oh, you're spoken for! What a pity. I thought my toy-boy had arrived.

Gerald Haven't you two met before?

Isobel No. I wasn't invited to the wedding. Remember? (*Looking at Mark
approvingly*) I'm sure I wouldn't have forgotten. Hallo, Mark.

They shake hands

Mark Hallo — er — (*he hesitates*) do *you* have a name?

Isobel Oh, yes. My parents gave me one of those when I was born. I'm just
waiting to see if Gerry's going to tell you what it is.

Mark Why? Is it a secret?

Isobel I'm not sure ... (*She looks at Gerald with a smile*)

Gerald Oh — sorry! This is Isobel French. Helen and I knew Isobel millions
of years ago.

Mark She doesn't look too bad for a million-year-old lady.

Isobel Thank you, Mark.

Gerald Isobel kindly drove here to express her condolences.

Mark Ah! I *thought* I hadn't seen you at the funeral.

Isobel No. I'm afraid I wasn't *there*, either. Was I, Gerry?

Mark You weren't in Tanzania by any chance?

Isobel I don't even know where it is! (*She laughs*)

Gerald It was all my fault. I'd mislaid Isobel's address.

Mark (*noticing the level of Isobel's drink*) Can I freshen you up a little?

Isobel Oh, yes, I think you can!

Mark (*indicating her glass*) Gin, was it?

Isobel Oh — gin — yes. Thank you.

Gerald (*abruptly*) You don't want *another* one, do you?

Mark and Isobel look at Gerald in surprise

Isobel Well, I've only had *one* ... (*She looks bleakly at her glass*)

Gerald But you'll be driving home soon!

Isobel Will I?

Gerald (*to Mark*) You mustn't ply her with drinks when she's driving!

Mark I didn't know she was driving. I thought she'd only just arrived.

Isobel So did I ... !

Mark looks at Isobel, a little embarrassed by his father-in-law's manners

Mark I'll just make it a small one. (*He takes her glass*)

Isobel Not *too* small.

Mark One not-too-small-gin-and-tonic coming up! (*He starts to go*)
Isobel Just gin.
Mark (*hesitating*) Just gin? No — er ...?
Isobel No.
Mark Just gin. Right. (*He goes to get it*)

Isobel looks at Gerald, puzzled by his sudden change of manner

Isobel Is everything all right, Gerry?
Gerald Yes, Yes, I think so.
Isobel (*a little hurt*) I thought you said you were pleased to see an old friend at a time like this.
Gerald Yes. I was. I am!
Mark (*arriving*) Just gin!

Isobel accepts her glass, pleased by the level of gin

Isobel Thank you, Mark! (*To Gerald*) I like your son-in-law already. (*To Mark*) Cheers! (*She sips her replenished gin*)
Mark So how long is it since you saw each other?
Isobel Oh — a few years, I suppose.
Mark (*astonished*) A few years?
Isobel Yes. I'm afraid so.
Mark You live quite far away, then?
Isobel N-no. Not *very* far ...
Mark And yet you haven't kept in touch?
Isobel No, we — we do seem to have drifted apart a bit. (*She giggles, nervously*)

Mark looks puzzled

Gerald (*intervening abruptly*) Hadn't you better be on your way? (*He tries to urge her on her way*)
Mark Don't be daft, Gerry! She's only just arrived. You've got all those lost years to catch up on. And you said yourself that she shouldn't drive when she's been drinking. You'd better stay the night, Isobel!
Gerald She can't do that!
Mark Of course she can! She doesn't want to go rushing off when she's only just arrived. (*To Isobel*) You *can* stay, can't you?
Isobel Well — yes — I suppose so ... (*She looks at Gerald uncertainly*)
Gerald No, she can't! There isn't any room!
Mark Of course there's room! She can sleep in the spare room.
Gerald We haven't got a spare room!

Mark You've got five bedrooms at least.

Gerald I use one as a study.

Mark That still leaves four. (*To Isobel*) That's settled, then. You're staying the night. (*To Gerald*) What would Helen have said if she'd known you were being inhospitable to an old friend?

Gerald That's not the point — — !

Isobel Don't you *want* me to stay, Gerry?

Mark Of course he does! And Shirley will be delighted. She's cooking a big meal tonight so there'll be plenty to go around.

Gerald (*to Mark, abruptly*) Hadn't you better go and see what's happening in the kitchen?

Mark (*rather surprised by this sudden non-sequitur*) I thought Shirley was seeing to that.

Gerald Well, she can't see to it *alone*, can she?

Mark Can't she?

Gerald Shirley needs help when she's cooking, doesn't she?

Mark Yes, I know that, but — —

Gerald Then go and see how she's getting on! (*He urges Mark towards the kitchen*)

Mark But Shirley's upstairs.

Gerald Well, there's *something* in the kitchen that you can sort out on your own, isn't there? (*Secretively*) I want to have a word with Isobel. (*He nods encouragingly*)

Mark (*delighted by Gerald's apparent recollection of his good manners*) That's more like it, Gerry! And about time, too! (*He chuckles, happily*) I'll leave you both to get down to the nitty-gritty, then. (*To Isobel, mysteriously*) I'm just going to — (*he gestures, vaguely*) sort something out in the kitchen.

Mark winks at Gerald and goes into the kitchen

Isobel goes to Gerald, puzzled by his strange behaviour

Isobel Are you *sure* you're all right?

Gerald Yes. I think so. Why?

Isobel You seem very anxious to get rid of me all of a sudden. I thought we were going to have a nice chat about the old days.

Gerald (*embarrassed*) Yes. We were ...

Isobel Mark and Shirley will think it very strange if I go shooting off when I've only just arrived.

Gerald Yes, I suppose they will ...

Isobel If there's a problem about me staying the night I can easily book a hotel.

Gerald Good idea! There's one just down the road. You can stay there and drive home first thing in the morning. (*He tries to lead her away*)

Isobel (*resisting*) Gerry! I can't go without saying hallo to Shirley. Whatever's she *doing* alone upstairs all this time?

Gerald She's not alone. That's the trouble! There — there's somebody up there with her.

Isobel Oh, I see! She's got a friend staying. *That's* why you were worried about the sleeping arrangements. Well, aren't I allowed to meet this friend of hers?

Gerald It's not a friend of hers.

Isobel Who is it, then?

Gerald says nothing

Gerry!

Gerald It's nobody *you* want to meet!

Isobel How do you know?

Gerald Because *I* know who it is! And it's nobody *you* want to meet.

Isobel I might.

Gerald You won't!

Isobel Why not?

Gerald (*with difficulty*) Because she's a — a person who likes asking questions. Likes poking her nose in. Not unkindly. She's not an unkind person.

Isobel And you think she might ask *me* questions?

Gerald I'm certain of it.

Isobel How can you be certain?

Gerald Because she's my sister-in-law.

Isobel *Amanda?*

Gerald Yes. Did you ever meet her?

Isobel No. I don't think so.

Gerald You'd remember if you had! And I don't want her cornering you and giving you the third degree.

Isobel Why should she do that?

Gerald She can't help herself! She's just interested in other people's private lives.

Isobel You mean she might start asking things about Alan? Why we broke up and all that.

Gerald Yes. I think she was suspicious at the time. Often asked loaded questions. And one thing might lead to another — and you might get upset all over again. And I don't want that. Not when you were kind enough to call with your condolences.

Isobel (*moved*) Aah … Fancy you thinking of that.

Gerald (*a little sheepish*) That was why I didn't want you to stay and sleep in the spare room.

Isobel Oh, Gerry. You are kind. (*She kisses him fondly on the cheek*)

Mark returns from the kitchen and sees the kiss

Mark There's nothing to sort out really. It … it looks like a stew. No sign of Shirl?

Gerald Not yet.

Mark I'll go and tell her that Isobel's here. (*He starts to go*)

Gerald No!

Mark (*hesitating*) No?

Gerald Isobel's not staying!

Mark Of course she's staying!

Gerald She only popped in to deliver her condolences and now she's delivered them she's going.

Isobel Yes. I really must fly! (*She hastily finishes her gin and tonic*)

Mark But I thought you were staying the night.

Gerald She's changed her mind.

Isobel Yes. I'm going to stay at a hotel down the road.

Mark You don't have to do that. I'm sure you two have a lot to say to each other after all these years.

Gerald We've already said it!

Mark She's only been here five minutes.

Isobel We're very fast talkers.

Mark But you haven't even seen Shirley yet!

Gerald She can see her another time.

Isobel Yes. And now I really must go!

Mark Surely you can at least stay for dinner?

Gerald She doesn't want any dinner!

Mark But she must be very hungry by now. You get very hungry driving a car for miles and miles.

Gerald She can take some smoked salmon sandwiches with her. I'm sure we can find some smoked salmon sandwiches somewhere, can't we? (*He starts to look under the sofa*)

Mark (*pulling him up, abruptly*) Isobel French didn't come all this way just for smoked salmon sandwiches!

Isobel No — I didn't! I'm not a *bit* hungry!

Mark (*unable to understand her reluctance to stay*) But Shirley's cooking dinner!

Isobel That's very nice of her, but — —

Mark And she'd *want* you to stay!

Shirley comes in from the hall and sees Isobel

Shirley Oh. Sorry. I didn't know anyone was here.
Isobel (*modestly*) It was only me.
Gerald You remember Isobel, darling?
Shirley Yes. Of course. (*Moving to Isobel*) It's been a long time.
Isobel Yes ... (*They embrace*) It's good to see you again.
Shirley I'm sorry. I didn't know that you were here.
Mark She was in the garden and spotted your father through the window.
Shirley Good heavens ... ! (*She giggles*)
Isobel Mark makes it sound more intriguing than it was. I ... I was so sorry
     to hear about your mother.
Shirley Thank you ...
Gerald Isobel came to express her sympathy.
Shirley That was kind of you.
Isobel And Gerry insisted that I stayed and had a drink.
Shirley (*laughing*) I should jolly well hope so!
Gerald And now she's leaving.
Mark No, she's not! There'll be plenty of stew for one more, won't there,
     Shirl?
Shirley Yes. Of course. (*To Mark, aside*) It's a casserole ... !
Gerald Isobel's not staying for dinner. You've only catered for three and
     there are four of us already.
Mark (*reassuringly*) It's all right. It's only a stew — and stews spread!
Shirley (*livid*) It's not only a stew! It's a casserole! With *herbs*!

Mark is a little taken aback by this unexpected outburst

Mark Sorry ...
Gerald (*to Isobel*) Come along! I'll take you into the dining-room!
Mark Why should she go into the dining-room if she isn't staying for dinner?
Gerald Because that's where the telephone lives.
Isobel In the dining-room?
Gerald I know it's unusual, but that's where we keep it. We'll telephone the
     hotel down the road and book you a room. And I'm sure you'll get a decent
     dinner *there*!

*Gerald grabs Isobel's hand and drags her out into the hall, closing the door
behind them*

Mark watches them go in surprise

Mark I can't think what's got into your father tonight!
Shirley (*seething*) Why can't you call it a casserole?
Mark (*lost for a moment*) Sorry?
Shirley It's not a "stew". It's a casserole! What will Isobel think? She drives
     here to express her condolences and you offer her a "stew"!

Mark (*defensively*) And gin!

Shirley That's not the point! It's a casserole. I'm cooking it in a bloody Le Creuset! That's what makes it a casserole!

Mark Oh. Right. My mistake. Sorry. It's a casserole. Fine. But it'll still *spread* surely?

Shirley (*her mind already elsewhere*) I hope Daddy's not going to let Isobel go without meeting Aunt Amanda. It'll seem so rude, Isobel being an old family friend and all that.

Mark An old family friend they hadn't *seen* for ages!

Shirley I can't think why he's trying to get rid of her.

Mark And *she* didn't seem eager to hang about, did she? One minute she's quite keen to stay the night and the next she can't wait to get out of here.

Shirley Amanda'll be down in a minute. She'll think it a bit odd if she sees Daddy disappearing down the garden dragging Isobel behind him. Whatever's going on?

Mark Perhaps he doesn't want Amanda to know that Isobel was here.

Shirley Don't be daft! Why should he want to keep her a secret?

Mark That's what *I'm* wondering ... ! And I'll tell you something else. Just now I came back in from the kitchen — and she was kissing him!

Shirley holds his look for a moment

Shirley What were you doing in the kitchen?

Mark What does it matter what I was doing in the kitchen?

Shirley Were you checking up on my casserole?

Mark Of course I wasn't!

Shirley I'm in charge of the casserole! The casserole is *my* prerogative!

Mark Yes. I know, but Gerry told me to go into the kitchen and see if there was anything I could do. So I went.

Shirley And when you came back she was kissing him?

Mark Yes.

Shirley (*after a moment's thought*) Was it a very long kiss?

Mark I'm not sure ...

Shirley Well, was it a quick peck or a long snog?

Mark I don't know! It was just finishing when I arrived. It's the *fact* of the kiss that's important, not its duration!

Shirley So it could just have been a quick peck?

Mark Yes. I suppose so.

Shirley A sympathetic old friend's peck?

Mark Possibly.

Shirley Well, that's all right, then, isn't it?

Mark You're taking all this very calmly. Gerry's only just buried your mother and already he's receiving kisses from old friends.

Shirley *One* old friend. And one quick peck.

Mark *And* he's trying to get that old friend out of the house before his sister-in-law sees her!

Shirley You've got a very suspicious mind.

Mark I'm not surprised! (*He has a sudden thought*) Here! Maybe there's something about Isobel that he doesn't want Amanda to find out.

Shirley What sort of thing?

Mark Maybe they had an affair.

Shirley Isobel and Daddy?

Mark Back in the Dark Ages. Why not? Come to think of it, they did look a bit guilty.

Shirley Don't be daft. He's a grandfather. Grandfathers don't have affairs!

Mark Well, there's *something* he doesn't want Amanda to know about. That's why he's trying to pack Isobel off to an hotel before Amanda can start firing questions. Maybe she's still after him!

Shirley Isobel? After Daddy?

Mark Why not?

Shirley Don't be silly. He's got his bus pass.

Mark Well, he's carrying on like a guilty husband in a French farce! And *she* didn't hang about, did she? Getting here. They haven't seen each other for years, but the minute she hears about Helen she drives over and starts drinking his gin.

Shirley That doesn't mean she fancies him! Honestly, Mark, you've lost the plot. How could anyone fancy Daddy?

Mark Your mother did.

Shirley That was different. They were younger then. Anyway, Isobel's married.

Mark We don't *know* that, do we?

Shirley What do you mean? I was at her wedding.

Mark She may have been married once. It doesn't mean that she's married now. She could be divorced, for all we know, and now she's on the look-out for a replacement.

Shirley (*laughing at the thought*) Don't be daft! Mummy's only been buried a week. Isobel would leave it a bit longer than *that* before throwing her cap in the ring!

Mark Why? You can't hang about, you know! Not if you're a divorcee. Haven't you noticed how few widowers there are living on their own around here? I tell you, it's a seller's market!

Shirley Mark!

Mark I tell you what, though — families ought to stick together. So if Gerry wants to keep Isobel a secret that's *his* business and we've got to back him up.

Shirley What are you talking about now?

Mark Well, we don't want to drop him in it, do we? So if Amanda starts asking questions about Isobel we'll have to cover for him.

Shirley Cover for him?

Mark Yes! We mustn't let Amanda know that Isobel has got her feet under the table.

Shirley But she hasn't!

Mark She soon *will* have!

Shirley If anyone's got their feet under the table it's Amanda! *She's* already moved in. *And* with two suitcases.

Mark (*realizing*) Hey — yes! You don't suppose *Amanda's* thinking of making a move on Gerry as well?

Shirley (*amused by the thought*) No, of course not! He's her brother-in-law.

Mark Well, you never know with these old people. Needs must when the devil drives!

They both laugh

> *Amanda returns. She has changed into a dress that is less severe than her previous outfit. She is rather surprised to find them laughing*

Amanda Isn't it rather unseemly to have such hilarity in a house of the mourning?

Shirley Yes. Of course. Sorry, Aunt Amanda. (*She assumes a more solemn mien*)

Mark puts his arm around Shirley

Mark It's just nerves. Stress. You know how it is. (*He comforts her elaborately*)

Shirley (*suddenly noticing*) You've changed!

Mark What?

Shirley She's changed!

Mark Has she? (*He looks and sees*) Good heavens! So she has ... ! (*He looks suspiciously at Amanda*)

Amanda I felt rather over-dressed with Gerry in that frightful jacket. (*She changes the subject abruptly*) Whatever's going on in the dining-room?

Shirley and Mark look at each other, uncertainly, then back at Amanda

Mark Sorry?

Amanda Gerry's in the dining-room with a strange woman.

Shirley and Mark exchange another look

Mark What?
Amanda Mark, are you deaf all of a sudden?
Shirley You — you mean you didn't recognize her?
Amanda I've never seen her before in my life.
Mark (*quietly*) Oh, good … !
Amanda What are they doing in the dining-room?
Shirley (*to Mark*) What are they doing in the dining-room?
Mark Ah. Yes. (*To Amanda*) Well, you see, she was outside — walking along the road — quite slowly as a matter of fact — —
Shirley And she saw Daddy through the window!
Amanda Why was she walking along the road looking through people's windows?
Mark Her telephone's out of order.

Shirley hides a giggle

Amanda I didn't know Gerry was a telephone engineer.
Mark No, no! She … she wanted to borrow Gerry's. To report it.
Shirley And that's what she's doing in the dining-room.
Amanda Borrowing Gerry's?
Mark Telephone. Yes. To report the fault.
Amanda Funny place to keep a telephone.
Mark Yes. I keep telling him he should have a mobile but he refuses.
Amanda I see …

Gerald returns with Isobel, talking as they arrive

Gerald It's no good. They can't help us. (*He sees Amanda*) I thought you were upstairs! Dinner isn't ready yet!
Amanda (*surprised by this*) Gerry! I couldn't stay up there forever! Did you ring the engineers?
Gerald (*blankly*) Sorry?

Amanda crosses to Isobel with a polite smile

Amanda I presume you are with British Telecom? They're usually very good in an emergency.
Isobel (*puzzled*) What emergency?
Gerald (*to Mark*) They were all booked up.
Amanda Don't be ridiculous! They can't *all* be booked up.
Gerald What?
Shirley (*to Isobel*) Does that mean that you *will* stay for dinner?
Isobel I — I'm not sure …

Amanda (*to Gerald, aside*) She came to borrow the telephone and now she's staying for dinner?

Gerald Why should she want to borrow the telephone?

Amanda (*turning back to Isobel*) How long have you been out of order, then?

Isobel Sorry?

Amanda You did come to borrow Gerry's?

Isobel (*all at sea*) Borrow Gerry's? (*She giggles*)

Mark (*hastily intervening*) About three hours! She was in the middle of an important conversation. (*Impressively*) To people in Padstow! Then the line went dead.

Isobel (*to Shirley*) I don't know anyone in Padstow …

Gerald What are you talking about?

Amanda Of course, if you're with one of those new firms then you've only got yourself to blame. I always stick to BT myself. And as far as I'm concerned mobiles are out of the question.

Isobel What exactly is it that I was going to borrow from Gerry?

Amanda His telephone, of course! Why else would you both be in the dining-room?

Isobel Sorry?

Amanda (*turning to Gerald*) That *was* why you were in the dining-room, wasn't it? To use the telephone?

Gerald Well, yes, but — —

Amanda Because *her* telephone is out of order?

Isobel (*looking up in surprise*) It's not, is it?

Amanda Of course it is!

Isobel Oh. (*To Shirley*) I didn't know that.

Amanda That was why you were walking up and down the street looking into people's houses! You were trying to find someone to borrow one from!

Mark turns to Shirley, anxious to escape

Mark (*quietly*) I think we'd better go and see to the stew! (*He leads her towards the kitchen*)

Shirley (*hissing at him angrily, as they go*) Why do you keep calling it a stew? It's a bloody casserole … !

Mark and Shirley go into the kitchen

Isobel (*amused at the thought*) I wasn't walking up and down the street! I came here by car.

Amanda I can't understand why you had to drive somewhere to borrow a telephone. Haven't you got neighbours where you live?

Isobel But I *didn't* come here to borrow the telephone!
Amanda You didn't?
Isobel No!
Gerald Are you sure?

Isobel looks at him in surprise

Isobel What?
Gerald (*clutching at straws*) Well, I suppose you *might* have come to borrow the telephone.
Isobel Might I?
Gerald (*with a shrug*) Why not?
Amanda Mark said you did.
Gerald Did he?
Amanda And if you didn't come here to borrow the telephone what *did* you come here for?

Isobel and Gerald exchange a look, realizing that there is now no escape

Isobel I ... I was visiting ...
Amanda Visiting? Then why did Mark tell me that tale about the telephone?
Gerald I can't imagine ... !
Amanda Well, then, Gerry — aren't you going to introduce me to your — visitor?
Gerald Ah. Yes. Of course. This is Isobel French.
Amanda Aaah! So *you're* Isobel French!
Isobel Yes ...
Gerald She's an old friend of ours.
Amanda Yes. I know. I've heard all about her.
Isobel H-have you?
Gerald She came to offer her condolences.
Amanda And do you always receive condolences in the dining-room?
Gerald Sorry?
Amanda You were both in the dining-room.
Gerald Ah. Yes. I was telephoning the hotel down the road. Isobel needs a room.
Amanda For what purpose, may I ask?
Gerald To stay the night!
Amanda (*to Isobel*) You don't live around here, then?
Isobel No. Not any more. And it's a bit far to drive back tonight now that Gerry's given me a couple of gins. (*She smiles guiltily*)
Gerald Only very small ones!
Amanda I see. And there's no room at the inn?
Gerald No. They're fully booked.

Amanda turns back to Isobel with a gracious smile

Amanda Then Isobel must stay here.
Gerald She can't!
Amanda Of course she can. She must. She certainly mustn't drive after gin.
Even very small ones.
Isobel So — you're Helen's sister, then?

Amanda looks at her for a moment, temporarily wrong-footed

Amanda How did *you* know who *I* was when *I* didn't know who *you* were?
Isobel Oh … Gerry told me that you were upstairs.
Amanda Then he should have told me that you were downstairs. (*She gives
Gerald a severe look*) You should have called me at once, Gerry. If I'd
known that an old family friend was here I'd have come straight down. (*To
Isobel*) I'm so sorry. You must have thought me very rude. I was changing
for dinner, you see.
Gerald (*noticing*) Good heavens, so you were … !
Amanda Well, I felt a sombre suit was a little out of place as you seemed
to be dressed for the golf course. I would have come down straight away
if I'd known Isobel was here. I hope you weren't thinking of packing her
off to an hotel without introducing us.
Gerald No! No — of course not — — !
Amanda That would have been such a pity when I've heard so much about
her. I'm sure we're going to find lots of things to talk about. (*To Isobel*) You
can tell me everything that went on in the good old days when you lived
just round the corner. So that's settled, Gerry. Isobel's staying for dinner.
Gerald There isn't enough!
Amanda Of course there's enough. I've had Shirley's casseroles before and
there's *always* enough.
Isobel No, I can't stay — really — — !
Amanda Of course you can!
Isobel I'd really rather drive home before it gets dark — — !
Amanda There's no question of you driving home now that Gerry's been
plying you with gin. Not only must you stay for dinner but you must stay
the night here, as well. She must stay the night here, mustn't she, Gerry?
Gerald Well, actually, I don't think — —
Isobel There isn't any room!
Amanda Nonsense. There are five bedrooms upstairs and only three appear
to be occupied. So that's settled, then! You'll stay the night here.
Isobel No — no, I couldn't, really — — !
Amanda Gerry insists! Don't you, Gerry?
Gerald Do I?
Amanda Of course you do! And more importantly — so do *I!*

Shirley and Mark come in from the hall

Shirley Come along, everybody! Dinner's ready!
Mark (*without enthusiasm*) Yes. Dinner's ready …
Amanda Oh, how lovely! Come along, Isobel! You're going to sit next to *me!* (*To Shirley and Mark, as she steers Isobel towards the hall*) And you don't have to worry about Isobel driving home because it's all been settled. She's going to stay *here* for the night!

Amanda sweeps Isobel out into the hall

Gerald glances briefly at Shirley and Mark and follows the ladies off, his head bowed

Mark and Shirley look at each other, giggle apprehensively and follow Gerald off

The Lights fade to Black-out

The CURTAIN *falls*

ACT II

The same. After dinner the same evening. It is now starting to get dark outside as the sun sets

When the CURTAIN *rises the hall light is on but the drawing-room lights are not*

The door to the hall opens and Gerald comes in. He sighs with relief, glad to have escaped from the dinner table. He shuts the door and hastens across to the drinks table. He switches on the lamp and quickly pours himself a brandy. He is about to drink it when the door opens again and Mark comes in, pursuing him, and switches the main lights on

Gerald quickly drinks his brandy and puts down the glass, hoping not to have been seen

Mark Gerry!
Gerald (*innocently*) Yes?
Mark (*going to Gerald*) What were you up to?
Gerald (*indicating his glass*) It was only a small one.
Mark In *there*! Shirley might have noticed!
Gerald Noticed what?
Mark You! Chasing the same piece of meat around your plate for a quarter of an hour.
Gerald You shouldn't have let her give me so much ... (*He sits on the sofa, sulking suitably*)
Mark I couldn't stop her! When Shirley starts serving stew she's like a woman on a mission.
Gerald Still, you did manage to remove both our unfinished plates without her noticing! That takes some doing. How on earth do you manage it?
Mark Years of practice! (*He sits next to Gerald*)

They both laugh

Gerald (*after a moment*) Trouble is — I'm still a bit peckish.
Mark So am I ... !

They both stare ahead in gloomy silence for a moment. Then they think of something and turn, in unison, to look at each other

Gerald Are *you* thinking what *I'm* thinking?
Mark (*enthusiastically*) Yes … !

Mark bends down and retrieves the smoked salmon sandwiches from their hiding place beneath the sofa. They each take a sandwich and grin at each other — mischievous schoolboys

Gerald That's more like it! Cheers!

They "toast" each other with their sandwiches and eat contentedly. After a moment Mark starts to pry, casually

Mark So … your old friend Isobel is staying the night, then?
Gerald She's not *my* old friend. She's *our* old friend.
Mark But she's still staying the night?
Gerald (*munching*) Apparently.
Mark Not quite what was planned, eh?
Gerald Well, you know what Amanda's like.
Mark I'm beginning to find out! You … you didn't *want* her to stay, though, did you?
Gerald Who?
Mark Isobel! To stay the night. You weren't very keen.
Gerald Wasn't I?
Mark Well, that was the impression *I* got! You rushed her out into the dining-room to phone a hotel. You practically dragged her out there!
Gerald Into the dining-room?
Mark You didn't even want her to stay for dinner! Even though she'd driven miles and miles to see you. You told her she could get a meal at the hotel!
Gerald Ah — yes. Tricky one, that … (*He escapes with his sandwich and turns on the desk lamp*)
Mark (*smiling, conspiratorially*) Was there … a good reason for that?
Gerald H'm? For what?
Mark For wanting Isobel to eat at the hotel! Surely it wasn't just to protect her from Shirley's cooking?
Gerald (*amused by the thought*) Oh, no! No — nothing like that. Oh, dear … ! Ha! Ha! (*He studies his sandwich*) These are rather good. I hope you remember where you bought them. We must have some more another time.
Mark (*continuing inexorably*) It was almost as if you didn't want Amanda to know about Isobel being here.
Gerald Really? (*He concentrates on his sandwich*)
Mark Well, that's what Shirley and I thought, anyway!
Gerald (*realizing*) Oh, I see! (*Resuming his seat*) *That* was why you made up that story about Isobel coming to borrow the telephone?

Mark Yes!

Gerald I did wonder …

Mark We were trying to help you out. That's what families are for, Gerry. To help out in a crisis.

Gerald I didn't know there *was* a crisis!

Mark Of course there's a crisis!

Gerald Oh. Well, that was very good of you. Very considerate. Thank you very much. Most ingenious.

Mark So … so that was it, then? (*He grins at Gerald triumphantly*) You didn't want Amanda to know that Isobel was here?

Gerald Well, you know what Amanda's like! She does tend to ask about other people's private lives. She can't help herself. And some people might not like that.

Mark *Some* people? You mean your old friend Isobel?

Gerald She's not *my* old friend. That would give the wrong impression. She's *our* old friend. Helen's and mine. (*He helps himself to another sandwich*)

Mark So it might be embarrassing?

Gerald (*busy eating*) Embarrassing?

Mark For Isobel! If Amanda stared firing questions at her.

Gerald Well — it might be, I suppose.

Mark Why? Has she got a cupboard full of skeletons?

Gerald Amanda?

Mark Isobel!

Gerald Oh. No, I don't think so. Well — not a cupboard full. I mean, we all have a few, don't we?

Mark So why should she be embarrassed?

Gerald You're asking a lot of questions.

Mark I just want to know why you were so keen to stop Amanda giving Isobel the third degree.

Gerald Well, Isobel doesn't want people prying into her affairs, does she?

Mark smiles, confident that he is now getting to the truth of the matter

Mark (*hopefully*) Has she had any, then?

Gerald What?

Mark Affairs!

Gerald *I* don't know, do I?

Mark You don't?

Gerald No! Of course not.

Mark (*disappointed*) Oh … So you and Isobel — haven't got a guilty secret, then? Something you don't want your sister-in-law to find out about?

Gerald A guilty secret? Me and Isobel? Good Lord, no! Whatever gave you that idea?

Mark Oh — nothing … (*He stares ahead, gloomily*)

Gerald (*patting Mark on the knee; gratefully*) Jolly good of you to help me out with that telephone story, though! (*He chuckles and finishes his sandwich*)

Amanda looks in from the kitchen

Amanda Black or white coffee, boys?

Gerald hastily hides the packet of sandwiches under his arms. Amanda notices this and moves behind the sofa to get a better look

  Gerry! What on earth are you doing?

Gerald Nothing!

Amanda You're crouched like a bird of prey. Are you hiding something?

Gerald No!

Mark Of course he's not!

Amanda looks between Gerald and Mark, suspiciously

Amanda You're like a pair of conspirators. Shirley wants to know if you want black or white coffee.

Gerald ⎫
          ⎬ (*together*) Yes, please!
Mark ⎭

Amanda Which?

Gerald Oh — er — black, please.

Mark Yes — fine — black. (*A sudden thought*) Ah! Just a minute. *I'll* do it! (*He gets up and starts to go*)

Gerald (*rising in alarm*) Where are you going?

Mark (*hesitating*) To tell Shirl about the coffee.

Gerald But Amanda was doing that!

Amanda You're not frightened of being left alone with me, are you, Gerry?

Gerald No! No — of course not. But Mark doesn't have to do it. He's been at work all day.

Mark (*pointedly*) But, Gerry — I need to … empty the *kitchen waste bin*, don't I?

Which surprises Amanda a little

Gerald Do you?

Mark Well, if they're washing up we don't want them to find the *kitchen waste bin* has been left full, do we?

Gerald (*catching on at last*) Ah — no — right! See what you mean.

Mark (*moving to Gerald*) I'll take that lot while I'm at it, shall I? (*He indicates the hidden sandwiches*)

Gerald Sorry?
Mark If I'm going outside to the dustbin.
Gerald (*realizing*) Ah — yes — right.

Mark closes to Gerald as if they are about to dance. They pass the package of remaining sandwiches from one to the other, trying to hide it from Amanda. Amanda watches them, puzzled by this extraordinary performance

   Having secured the package under his arms, Mark backs towards the kitchen door. He grins at Amanda self-consciously and hastens out

Amanda What on earth were you doing? You appeared to be playing pass the parcel.
Gerald It was just some bits of rubbish. As you girls were busy out there, we thought we'd tidy up a bit in here.
Amanda (*giving him a doubtful look*) I see ... (*She sits on the sofa*) I can't think why Mark told me that Isobel had come here to borrow the telephone.
Gerald Ah. Yes. That was a bit strange, wasn't it?
Amanda I felt such a fool. Isobel must have thought I was mad. Why should he make up a story like that?
Gerald I — I can't imagine ... A joke, possibly?
Amanda Don't be silly, Gerry. Mark doesn't do jokes.
Gerald No. Right.
Amanda It was almost as if he didn't want me to know about Isobel being here.
Gerald (*in massive disbelief*) Really? Good lord ... !
Amanda Well, that's what it seemed to me.
Gerald Yes. I suppose it *could* have sounded like that. I think I'll have a brandy. (*He hastens away to pour a brandy*)
Amanda I mean, I was bound to meet her sooner or later, she being an old friend and all that. Obviously our paths are bound to cross, now that I'm a fixture as it were.
Gerald (*unhappily*) Yes. Bound to ...
Amanda So there's no reason why I shouldn't meet her, is there?
Gerald None that *I* know of.
Amanda She seems very nice. Even if she *is* drinking rather a lot of wine.
Gerald (*returning*) I expect she's embarrassed. People often turn to drink when they're embarrassed. Cheers. (*He sips his brandy*)
Amanda Isobel must have thought that you were very rude.
Gerald (*puzzled by this change of direction*) Sorry?
Amanda Not offering her a bed for the night. What would Helen have thought? *She* was always so hospitable. I presume she was at the funeral?
Gerald Helen? Yes, of course she was! (*He laughs*)

Amanda (*giving him a pained look*) Not Helen! Isobel! Presumably *she* was at the graveside?

Gerald Ah. No. I'm afraid not.

Amanda (*shocked*) Not at the graveside?

Gerald Well, neither were you! And you're her sister.

Amanda Only because I got the wrong date. Really, Gerry, you mustn't hold that against me. I made a mistake. We all make mistakes. But I'm surprised Isobel wasn't there, she being an old friend and all that.

Gerald She didn't hear about it until it was too late.

Amanda You mean you didn't tell her?

Gerald No. I forgot.

Amanda Forgot? You should have made a list. On these occasions one should make a funeral list in the same way one makes a wedding list.

Gerald And leave a present list at Harrods?

Amanda Now you're being facetious, Gerry, and it doesn't suit you. All the same, Isobel must have felt very neglected. No wonder she's plunging into the claret. You don't suppose Mark was trying to keep it from Isobel that I was staying here. And *that* was why he pretended that she'd come to borrow the telephone?

Gerald Why should he want to do that?

Amanda Surely she wouldn't think that there was anything unseemly about my moving in with you?

Gerald I wouldn't have thought so!

Amanda Anyway, he'd have been wasting his time because you must have already told Isobel that I was staying here.

Gerald Ah — yes ...

Amanda Gerry — — ?

Gerald What?

Amanda You did *tell* Isobel? About me staying here.

Gerald Ah. No. Not yet.

Amanda It's not a secret, is it?

Gerald No! Of course not! I — I just haven't had the chance.

Amanda Yes, you have. You could have told her during dinner.

Gerald Ah. Yes ...

Amanda But you didn't.

Gerald No ...

Amanda Gerry ... Is there something you haven't told me about Isobel?

Isobel looks in from the kitchen. She is now wearing an apron

Isobel Black or white coffee, Gerry?

Amanda He's already ordered!

Isobel Oh. Sorry. I didn't know.

Gerald I thought Mark was seeing to it.

Amanda I knew I should have done it myself! (*She starts to go, but hesitates near Isobel*) I think Gerry's got something he wants to tell you.

Amanda gives Gerald a severe look and marches out impatiently into the kitchen

Isobel pulls a face at Gerald

Isobel She's very bossy, isn't she?

Gerald I did warn you!

They both laugh

Isobel All through dinner she kept firing questions at me about my marriage to Alan.

Gerald Well, I told you she had an inquiring mind.

Isobel It was almost as if she knew what had happened. Helen wouldn't have *told* her, would she?

Gerald I hope not!

Isobel Luckily, Shirley was sitting next to me so I was able to change the subject and ask about her boys. You're very lucky having a daughter.

Gerald Yes. I know.

Isobel I envy you. I wish *I'd* had children.

Gerald Yes. It would have been nice.

Isobel Then — who knows? — I might still have been married to Alan. (*She sighs, a little sadly*) Oh, dear ... (*A beat, then she activates herself*) I'd better go and finish the drying up before Amanda starts complaining about that! (*She laughs and starts to go, then stops and looks back at Gerald*) What was it you wanted to tell me?

Gerald Oh — er — it wasn't important.

Shirley and Mark come in from the kitchen. He is carrying two cups of coffee

Isobel Lovely casserole, Shirley!

Shirley Oh — thank you.

Isobel Lovely casserole, wasn't it, boys?

Gerald }
Mark } (*together*) Yes ... !

Isobel You must let me have the recipe.

Shirley (*flattered*) Oh — right! And there's plenty left if you're still hungry.

Gerald Yes. You can take it home in a doggy bag.

Isobel is not sure how to take this. She giggles at Gerald and darts out into the kitchen

Mark hands a cup of coffee to Gerald

Mark One black coffee.
Gerald (*taking the coffee*) Thank you, Mark. (*Confidentially*) Everything ... all right out there? (*He nods in the direction of the kitchen*)
Mark (*grinning triumphantly*) Yes — everything under control!

They laugh together and Shirley looks at them suspiciously

Amanda bustles back in with her own cup of coffee

Amanda Did you *get* coffee, Gerry? (*She sees that he did*) Ah — yes.
Mark You see? I *can* manage a cup of coffee, Aunt Amanda. (*He grins at her*)
Shirley Yes. Mark's been very helpful in the kitchen. He even insisted on taking the rubbish out to the dustbin. Didn't you, darling?
Mark It was the least I could do. (*He exchanges a look with Gerald and goes to join Shirley*)
Amanda (*to Gerald*) Isobel's just finishing off the drying-up.
Gerald Good heavens, she doesn't have to do that.
Amanda Oh, don't worry. I'm sure she's finishing off the claret as well. (*She sits on the sofa*) So how did she react?
Gerald Who?
Amanda Isobel! Just now. When you told her.

Gerald remains silent

Gerry! You did *tell* her?
Gerald No. I — I didn't get the chance.

Isobel returns, having removed her apron, and almost managing to conceal the fact that she is a tiny bit the worse for wine

Ah — Isobel! You shouldn't be out there working. Come and sit down.
Amanda (*imperiously*) Yes. Come and sit down next to *me!*

Isobel exchanges a look with Gerald and then goes and sits reluctantly next to Amanda

I tried to speak to you during dinner but you kept changing the subject.

Isobel (*innocently*) Did I? I'm so sorry. I didn't mean to.

Amanda There's something I've been simply longing to ask you about.

Gerald Isobel came here to offer her condolences not to answer a lot of questions!

Amanda I'm only interested, Gerry. Isobel knows that.

Isobel (*seizing the initiative*) I'm so glad you were able to be at the funeral, Amanda. You must have been a great comfort to Gerry.

Which puts Amanda on the back foot for a moment

Amanda Ah. Well ...

Shirley You weren't there, were you, Aunt Amanda?

Amanda gives Shirley a look. Isobel reaps the benefit of this information

Isobel Not at your own sister's funeral?

Amanda I — I thought it was *this* Saturday.

Isobel Gerry! You didn't tell her the wrong date?

Gerald No, of course I didn't!

Amanda I couldn't have been here last week anyway.

Isobel How inconsiderate of Helen! She should have hung on until it was more convenient for you. So where *were* you last week?

Amanda In Tanzania.

Isobel Don't they have aircraft in Tanzania?

Gerald (*hiding his amusement*) I'm sure Amanda came as quickly as she could.

Isobel (*to Amanda*) So when *did* you get here?

Amanda Today.

Isobel So you've only just arrived?

Amanda Yes. I'm afraid I got my dates mixed up.

Isobel You mean you had more than *one* sister to bury?

Gerald snorts

Amanda Now you're being facetious, Isobel. Anyway, I understand that *you* weren't at the funeral either.

Isobel No. I'm afraid I wasn't ...

Gerald With neither of you there I'm surprised *Helen* bothered to turn up!

Gerald and Mark enjoy the joke

Shirley Daddy ... !

Gerald Sorry. (*He looks suitably ashamed*)

Amanda I was upstairs unpacking when you arrived.
Isobel Unpacking?
Amanda Gerry — I think this is the moment you've been waiting for. You'd better tell her now.
Isobel Tell me what? (*She looks at Gerald*)

Gerald exchanges a look with Amanda

Gerald Amanda's going to stay here.
Isobel *Stay* here? With *you*?
Gerald Yes ...
Isobel How long for?
Gerald The rest of my life, apparently.
Isobel (*unable to contain her amusement*) Good heavens! (*To Amanda*) I assumed you were just staying overnight like me. I didn't realize you were going to be a fixture!
Shirley Apparently, it was what Mummy said she wanted.
Isobel For Amanda to become a fixture?
Amanda I promised Helen that I'd look after Gerry if anything happened to her.
Isobel For the rest of his life?
Amanda Yes.
Gerald It was all settled over coffee in Selfridges.
Isobel You mean you didn't know about this little arrangement?
Gerald Well — er — no, not exactly ...
Isobel Poor Gerry ... ! You must have been very surprised when your sister-in-law arrived with heavy baggage.
Gerald (*quietly*) Yes. I *was* ... !
Shirley We did ask Daddy to live with *us*.
Gerald Yes! And I said that I would!
Amanda And *I* said that that was quite out of the question.
Mark Actually, Amanda, I think Gerry would prefer to live on his own.
Gerald Yes, I — —
Amanda Nonsense! He'd be helpless on his own! We all know that. That's why Helen insisted that I make this promise. (*Decisively*) And it's a promise that I intend to keep.
Isobel You're not married, then?
Amanda No.
Isobel (*with a smile*) No live-in lover lurking?
Amanda Certainly not!
Isobel No wonder you came back from Tanzania and got your feet under the table.
Amanda I'm moving in with Gerry at the request of his late wife, not to satisfy my carnal desires.

Gerald I am still in the room, you know.

Isobel (*to Amanda*) I didn't realize that you were a spinster.

Amanda (*coldly*) I'm not a spinster. I'm single. It's quite different.

Isobel Oh — sorry ...

Amanda Don't be sorry. *I'm* not.

Gerald And it wasn't through lack of chances, was it, Amanda?

Amanda Thank you, Gerry. (*Continuing to Isobel*) I've managed to go through my entire life without forming a lasting relationship with a single member of the opposite sex. (*She smiles triumphantly*)

Shirley Good heavens ... ! (*She looks at Mark*)

Mark (*a sudden thought*) Amanda, you're not — — ?

Amanda No, I am not! And having got thus far in life on my own I do not intend to spoil my record by pursuing aged widowers!

Gerald I'm not an aged widower!

Amanda (*not unkindly*) Yes, you are, Gerry. You're nearly seventy and your wife's dead. That makes you an aged widower.

Gerald Oh. I hadn't thought of it like that ... (*With a wicked smile*) So you and I are a couple of old geriatrics, then?

Amanda (*not too keen*) Well — yes. I suppose we are. And I can assure you, Isobel, that I for one have no intention of trying to play new music on an old instrument.

The doorbell rings

Mark You're not expecting anyone *else* to arrive, are you, Gerry?

Gerald I hope not ... !

Mark Perhaps this time it really *is* the vicar.

Shirley I'll go and see.

Shirley runs out into the hall

Amanda I didn't know that you socialized with the clergy.

Gerald I don't usually. I only met him last week. And that was a special occasion.

Mark Really? What was that, then? (*Remembering*) Oh — yes ...

Shirley returns

Is it the vicar?

Shirley No. Mrs Capstick.

Amanda Who's Mrs Capstick?

Shirley Daddy's daily help. She comes in two or three times a week.

Amanda Not in the *evening*, surely?

Carol Capstick comes in. She is not what we expected: a very pretty girl in her thirties. With legs

Amanda and Isobel look at her in some surprise

Carol I hope I'm not disturbing you.
Gerald Not at all. Come on in, Carol!

Amanda reacts to this familiarity

Carol I was just passing so I thought I'd pop in and sort out the arrangement. I didn't know you were going to have company tonight.
Gerald Neither did I ... ! Let me introduce you. This is my sister-in-law, Amanda.
Carol Hallo, Amanda!
Amanda (*coldly*) How do you do, Mrs Capstick.
Carol I was so sorry about Helen. We got on really well. Just like friends. (*With a hint of criticism*) Pity you couldn't get to her funeral.
Amanda Yes ...
Carol Still, you're here now, eh? That's the main thing. And it's very nice of you to call.
Amanda I'm not just *calling*!
Carol (*puzzled*) Sorry?
Gerald (*hastily intervening*) And this is Isobel French. She's a very old friend of ours.
Isobel You don't have to make me sound a hundred! (*She moves to greet Carol*) Hallo, Carol. It's nice to meet you.

Isobel and Carol shake hands

Carol Nice to meet you too, Isobel. (*Gently remonstrating*) I don't remember seeing *you* at the funeral either!
Isobel No. I'm afraid I wasn't there ... (*She looks at Gerald, a little embarrassed*)
Amanda I assume that *you* were there, though, Mrs Capstick?
Carol Oh, yes! Had to see her off. Didn't I, Gerry?

Gerald nods, smiling warmly at Carol

Gerald Of course you did ...
Carol Oh, and I did cry! Didn't I, Gerry?
Gerald Yes. You certainly did! So did I ...

There is a brief moment of sadness between them

Carol Still, if you can't cry at a funeral when *can* you cry, eh? (*To Amanda*) I didn't wear black, mind.
Amanda Really?
Carol Oh, no. Helen wouldn't have liked that. I went like this, really. More or less. Informal. You know?
Amanda I can imagine …
Mark Let me get you a drink, Carol.
Carol Oh, no! No I couldn't do that.
Gerald Nonsense! We're delighted to see you. Aren't we, Mark?
Mark We certainly are! (*He grins a little too enthusiastically*)

Shirley gives Mark a look

Gerald Come and sit down.
Carol Oh. Right. Thanks, Gerry!

Carol sits down. There is a lot of leg. Isobel is amused. Amanda is not

Mark What'll it be then? G and T?
Carol Ooh, that would be nice!
Mark One G and T coming up! (*He goes to see to it*)
Isobel Was your husband at the funeral?
Carol Oh, no! He moved on a long time ago.
Amanda You mean *he's* deceased as well?
Carol No, no! He moved on through the divorce courts.
Amanda So now I presume you're on the look-out for another one?
Carol Not likely! Once was enough for me.

Mark arrives with the gin and tonic

Mark One G and T! (*He hands her the glass*)
Carol Thanks, Mark. (*She raises her glass*) Well — here's to Helen, eh, Gerry?
Gerald (*nodding; sadly*) Yes …

Carol reverently sips her drink

Isobel How long have you been working for Helen and Gerry, then?
Carol About eighteen months now, isn't it, Gerry? And I really like it here. Which is just as well, eh? In view of the new arrangement. (*She giggles*)
Gerald Oh. What new arrangement is that?
Carol Oh, Gerry, you are funny! You must know about the new arrangement.

Gerald Must I?

Carol Well, I'm staying with my mum at the moment, you see, but as soon as Shirley and Mark go back home I'll be packing my bags.

Gerald Packing your bags? Are you going somewhere?

Carol Of course I'm going somewhere! I'm coming here!

Gerald *Here*? You mean — "*here* here"?

Carol Yes.

Gerald But this is where *I* live.

Carol (*smiling; happily*) Well, why else do you think I'm coming here? (*Turning to Mark*) You certainly know how to mix a G and T, Mark. I'll say that for you. (*She plunges into her glass*)

Gerald Sorry, Carol, but I ... I am a little confused ...

Amanda So am I!

Gerald Why should you need to pack your bags to come here and clean? I'm sure we've plenty of dusters in the house.

Carol No, no! From now on I'm going to be living *in*!

They others all look at her in surprise

Gerald Living in?

Carol Yes.

Shirley and Mark exchange a look

Amanda A living-in daily lady?

Carol Didn't you know about it, Gerry?

Gerald No. I don't think I did ...!

Carol Helen never told you?

Gerald No. I don't recall it being mentioned ...

Carol But *you* knew, Shirley?

Shirley No. It's the first *I've* heard of it, too.

Carol Good heavens! Helen and me had a long talk about it!

Gerald In Selfridges, I suppose ...

Carol No, no! Here — in the kitchen — when we were having our elevenses. You *sure* she never told you about it?

Gerald I think I'd have remembered ...

Carol We had such a lovely discussion. I reckon Helen must have had a feeling about what was going to take place because she said that if anything happened to her would I promise to stay here and look after you. That's why I'm packing my bags — to move in here.

A moment's silence as they all digest this information

Shirley But you can't stay here with Daddy! It — it wouldn't be right.

Carol Why not?

Mark Well, for one thing he's an Old Age Pensioner!

Amanda Yes. He's far too old to have young girls in and out of the bathroom.

Gerald (*reasonably*) We have got *two* bathrooms ...

Shirley What does *that* mean?!

Gerald It doesn't mean anything! Just that we have two bathrooms. So the number of bathrooms isn't an issue.

Amanda But, Gerry, you're a — —

Gerald An ageing widower! Yes, you told me!

Carol What's age got to do with it?

Gerald Yes — exactly! See?

Isobel (*with a smile*) Did you plan all this, Gerry?

Gerald Of course I didn't!

Isobel Well, you don't seem to be against the idea.

Gerald I'm simply saying that age and bathrooms have nothing to do with the topic under discussion.

Carol You see? Gerry and I agree. We'll get on like a house on fire. Won't we, Gerry?

Amanda But what about the neighbours?

Gerald They're not moving in as well, are they?

Amanda What will they think? An old man and a young girl!

Isobel They'll probably ring up to congratulate him.

Gerald tries to regroup and takes Carol aside a little

Gerald Now — er — now, Carol — I think there has been a — a slight misunderstanding here ...

Carol There's no misunderstanding, Gerry. I promised Helen I'd stay here with you and that's that.

Gerald Ah — yes — but you see — when you and Helen had this discussion, and Helen said she wanted you to stay with me, what she probably meant was that she didn't want you to leave me in the lurch — as regards the domestic department. She simply meant for you to stay with me — as a cleaning lady. Meaning for two or three hours per diem. And then — to go home. You see? (*He smiles triumphantly*)

Carol You weren't there, Gerry. You didn't hear what Helen said.

Gerald No — no, I admit that, but — —

Carol Well, I was and I did! Cleaning and companionship. Those were her very words. And you can't have both of those if you're only here for two or three hours per diem, now can you?

Amanda Well, it's quite out of the question.

Carol Why?

Amanda Because *I'm* moving in with Gerry.

Carol looks at her in surprise

Carol *You?*
Amanda Yes.
Carol (*laughing*) Don't be silly, Amanda!
Amanda I am not being silly. I've already moved in.
Isobel Yes, she has! Her suitcases are upstairs.
Carol But what's the point of *you* moving in? *You're* not a cleaning lady.
Amanda No, I am not! But presumably *you'll* still be doing that.
Carol So what will *you* be doing?
Isobel That's what *I* was wondering … !

Amanda looks witheringly at Isobel

Amanda Isobel, you really must try to keep your mind above the level of the gutter.
Carol (*to Gerald*) Did you know that Amanda was moving in?
Gerald No, not exactly … !
Carol (*to Amanda*) There! He wasn't expecting you. So you don't have to bother. Me and Gerry can manage on our own.
Amanda No, you can't. I gave my word to Helen.
Carol And so did I! What about you, Isobel? *You're* not thinking of moving in as well, are you?
Gerald No, she is not! She's only here for the night.
Carol You should have told me you had two ladies staying the night.
Gerald I didn't know, did I?
Carol Lucky I popped in, then, wasn't it? I'll go up and see to the beds.
Amanda You don't have to do that! I *can* make up my own bed. Besides, you've got to stay down here. Gerry has got something he wishes to say to you.
Gerald Have I?
Amanda Yes! You've got to clear up the misunderstanding.
Gerald What misunderstanding?
Amanda The one concerning the living-in daily lady! (*She heads for the hall door*)
Carol (*following Amanda*) There's no misunderstanding concerning me! I'm moving in with Gerry and that's that!

Amanda goes, followed by Carol. Their disagreement continues off stage as they head for the stairs

Gerald looks miserably at the others

Gerald I can't have two women moving in and fighting over the washing machine. (*He heads for the hall door*) Carol! Amanda! Wait a minute! Can't we *talk* about this?

Gerald goes in despair, closing the door behind him

Isobel Poor Gerry …! (*She starts to collect the coffee cups*)
Shirley I wish Mummy hadn't been so keen on making lists … Isobel! What *are* you doing?
Isobel I thought I'd just take these out into the kitchen.
Shirley No! You've done quite enough already.
Isobel But I must do *something* to help, otherwise Amanda will start complaining again!

Isobel laughs and goes into the kitchen with the coffee cups

Mark What is it with your father?
Shirley What do you mean?
Mark He seems to have three women pursuing him! One married, one divorced and one neutral. That's not bad for nearly seventy, is it?
Shirley They're not pursuing him! They just want to look after him.
Mark Oh, yes?
Shirley Anyway, Carol's far too young to be chasing old age pensioners. And Amanda's not interested in men.
Mark She didn't say she wasn't interested. Just that she never had any.
Shirley She never wanted a serious relationship with the opposite sex. She said so.
Mark Well, if she wanted to keep up her record as an ageing spinster why did she bother to change for dinner? Yes! Maybe she *always* fancied your father!
Shirley Don't be daft! She changed her clothes because she wanted to relax, that's all.
Mark And what about Isobel? I bet *she* didn't come all this way just to offer her condolences! (*He grins at her*)
Shirley Nonsense! Isobel's just an old friend.
Mark I don't know about that. She was rather put out when she heard that Amanda was moving in. Quite sulky, in fact. And at dinner she was knocking back the claret like there was no tomorrow.
Shirley (*laughing*) That doesn't mean she fancies him.
Mark (*warming to his subject*) She hadn't seen your father for yonks, and yet she drives here just to express her condolences? She could have done that on the telephone. Or sent him an email. She couldn't wait to get her feet under the table!

Shirley She's only staying tonight!
Mark (*teasing*) That can be changed.
Shirley Anyway, I told you. She's already married.

Mark gives a doubtful look

Mark How can you be sure? Where is he? *He* hasn't driven miles and miles
  to express his sympathy, has he?
Shirley No, but — —
Mark I'll ask her!
Shirley No, you won't!
Mark Why not?
Shirley No!

Isobel returns

Mark Ah — Isobel! There you are! Come and sit down over here. (*He smiles
  encouragingly*)

Isobel sits down

Shirley gives Mark a warning glance

Isobel (*to Shirley*) Mrs Capstick was a bit of a surprise. I was quite taken
  aback. She's not exactly the traditional idea of a daily help, is she?
Shirley (*laughing, but keeping her eye on Mark*) No!

Mark closes in on Isobel, a beast stalking its prey

Mark Isobel — we — we were both wondering — —
Shirley No, we weren't!
Mark Yes, we were!
Isobel Wondering what?
Mark Whether you were — —
Shirley Mark … ! (*She gives him a severe look*)
Isobel (*amused*) Well, go on! You were wondering whether I was what?
Mark Married! Are you? Married? Er — *still* married? *Now*? Like you used
  to be?
Isobel Oh, no. Not any more.
Mark You're *not*? (*He glances at Shirley, his suspicions apparently
  confirmed*) Sorry, I — I didn't know that, you see. About you not being
  married. Sorry.
Isobel There's no need to apologize. I wasn't at all sorry to see the last one
  go.

Mark The — er — the *last* one?

Isobel Yes. Marrying him was the greatest mistake of my life.

Mark But — er — but you said — the — the *last* one?

Isobel Yes.

Mark When you say "last one" — er — does that mean the last one of *two*?

Isobel (*cheerfully*) Oh, no! The last one of three.

Mark Three?!

Isobel Yes.

Mark Oh. Right …

Mark and Shirley exchange a quick look

Isobel (*to Shirley, with a smile*) I needn't have worried about your father being alone, need I? He seems to have a *choice* of ladies wanting to look after him.

Shirley You *were* worried about him, then?

Isobel Of course. We're old friends.

Mark So — er — you've been married three times, then, Isobel? Well, well! (*He laughs nervously*) That's quite a record!

Shirley She doesn't want to talk about it!

Isobel That's all right, Shirley. I don't mind. After all, you'd have found out sooner or later, wouldn't you?

Shirley Would we?

Isobel Well — if I'm going to be around more often from now on.

Mark and Shirley exchange another look

Shirley And … and is that what you're going to be? Around more often? From now on?

Isobel I jolly well hope so! As Gerry said, you need old friends at a time like this.

Mark (*after a moment's hesitation*) So — er — what — what happened to the other two? Did you divorce *them*, as well?

Isobel Certainly!

Mark Yes. I see. Right …

Isobel Mind you, I hadn't known the second one very long. I rushed into it far too quickly after my first divorce.

Mark And rushed out equally quickly! (*He laughs*)

Isobel Still, he did give me rather a lot of money.

Mark stops laughing

Mark Did he? Oh. Good. That was some consolation.

Isobel Well, you can't let them get away without paying, can you? You remember that, Shirley, when *your* time comes!

Mark and Shirley are not sure if she is joking or not

Mark And did the other two part with plenty of dosh, as well?
Isobel Oh, yes! I was quite fortunate in that respect.
Mark I see ... (*Quietly*) Oh, my God ... !
Isobel Surely you don't disapprove, Mark?
Mark No — no, of course not!
Isobel You couldn't expect me to be divorced without a decent settlement, now could you?
Mark No — no, of course not! (*Trying to smile; jokingly*) So now I suppose you'll be on the look-out for a fourth?
Shirley (*horrified*) Mark!
Isobel I *might* be ...

Mark looks quickly at Shirley:"I told you so!"

After all, we girls don't give up, do we, Shirley? Even after a few bad experiences like I've had! (*Suddenly doubtful*) I'm not too old to hope for another one to come along, am I, Mark?
Mark No! No, of course not. Far from it.
Shirley But your *first* marriage wasn't a bad experience, was it? When you were seeing a lot of Mummy and Daddy. You were happily married *then,* weren't you? To Alan.
Isobel Oh, yes. *Very* happy ...
Mark Well, that's all right, then, isn't it? One out of three can't be bad! (*He laughs nervously*)
Isobel No ...

Then suddenly she is in tears and gets up and runs out into the garden

Shirley and Mark are left behind in a state of puzzled astonishment

Mark (*innocently*) What did I say?
Shirley You kept firing questions at her!
Mark She mentioned two bad marriages and managed not to cry *then.* Yet she bursts into tears when we mention the one good one!

Gerald comes back in from the hall, looking rather downcast

Gerald It's no good. They won't listen to me. I can't get a word in edgeways. (*Noticing Isobel's absence*) Isobel hasn't gone back on to the claret, has she?

Mark No. She ... she ran out into the garden.

Gerald (*cheering up*) You mean she's gone? Oh, well, that's one less to worry about ... !

Shirley Daddy! Isobel's an old family friend, and she came here to offer you comfort.

Mark And I bet that's not all!

Gerald Sorry?

Mark Gerry — she's a triple divorcee!

Gerald Yes. I know. She told me.

Mark Well, if *I* was a widower and a triple divorcee came to comfort me I'd be suspicious!

Shirley (*to Mark*) You'd better go and fetch her back.

Mark I think she wants to be alone.

Shirley Go and fetch her back! (*She gives Mark a push*)

Mark All right. But, remember — if this goes wrong it's all *your* fault!

Mark goes into the garden

Gerald looks puzzled

Gerald What's he on about?

Shirley Don't take any notice. He's always jumping to conclusions.

Gerald I don't understand. Why did she run out into the garden?

Shirley I think she's a little upset.

Gerald About what?

Shirley I'm not sure. She suddenly got up and ran out crying.

Gerald Well, what were you all talking about?

Shirley You know what Mark's like. He will keep asking questions.

Gerald Yes, I know ... !

Shirley He kept on asking about her marriages!

Gerald Ah ...

Shirley I didn't know that she'd had three of them.

Gerald Neither did I until today ... !

Shirley She seemed quite happy talking about the two bad ones, but when we asked about the good one she started to cry.

Gerald Oh, dear ...

Shirley (*noticing his tone of voice*) Daddy ... ?

Gerald H'm?

Shirley Is there something I don't know about Isobel?

Gerald No. No, of course not.

Shirley Why should she cry about the *happy* marriage?

There is a moment's pause

Mark brings Isobel back in from the garden. She has pulled herself together a bit

Isobel I'm so sorry, Shirley. What must you think of me? I'm afraid I've had a little too much to drink. Your wine was far too good, Gerry. And red wine always makes me maudlin.
Gerald Don't you worry. Come and sit down.

As Isobel sits on the sofa, Mark signals wildly to Gerald, trying to warn him about her intentions. Gerald is puzzled, not knowing the reason for this pantomime

Shirley I — I'd better go and see how Amanda and Carol are getting on upstairs. (*She heads for the door, then looks back at Mark*) You come with me, darling.
Mark What?

Shirley nods towards the sad figure on the sofa

(*Catching on*) Oh. Yes. Right.

Mark follows Shirley out into the hall, closing the door behind him

Gerald sits beside Isobel. She gives an embarrassed smile

Isobel I'm sorry ...
Gerald No need to be. They didn't mean to upset you.
Isobel No, of course they didn't. It was all my fault. I shouldn't have drunk so much. I've only myself to blame. But sometimes ... the memories come back. You know how it is.
Gerald Yes. Yes, I know ... But, you see, Shirley never knew about Alan and Helen.
Isobel I'm jolly glad she didn't! Daughters don't expect their aged mothers to have had affairs. Especially with the husband of their best friend. You won't ever tell her, will you?
Gerald No, of course not. It'll always be *our* secret. It was all a long time ago, anyway. Water under the bridge now. (*He leans forward a little to look at her, reassuringly*) It ... it wasn't important, you know. Not *really* important.
Isobel Wasn't it?
Gerald Well, it only lasted three months.
Isobel Is that all? It felt like three years. (*A pause*) And *you* were the lucky one!

Gerald Was I?

Isobel *You* were able to forgive.

Gerald Yes …

Isobel Did you never regret it?

Gerald Forgiving? No. Never. Helen and I had a very happy marriage. I wasn't going to let three crazy months spoil that. And *you* should have done the same! *You* should have forgiven *Alan!*

Isobel *Why?* He betrayed me!

Gerald Only for three months!

They laugh

They both regretted it, you know.

Isobel (*uncertainly*) *Did* they?

Gerald They realized that they'd made a mistake. These things happen. You have to get over them. Helen and I had been married for forty-five years when she died. So those three months hadn't made a hell of a lot of difference, had they?

Isobel No. No, I suppose not …

Gerald Because they weren't important.

Isobel holds his look for a moment

Isobel No. I suppose you're right. And I wish so much that Alan and I *had* got back together again. But at the time I — I just couldn't. And then he went and got married again and had two kids and it was all too bloody late! I just wish now that I *had* forgiven the bugger. Oh, hell! Why do I always mess up?

Gerald embraces Isobel comfortingly

Mark and Shirley return and see them. Not knowing the truth, they naturally jump to the wrong conclusion

Mark Oh — sorry!

Gerald and Isobel separate. Gerald rises, embarrassed, catches Mark's look and tries to appear innocent, shrugging it off. Shirley looks at her father, uncertain what this is all about

Shirley (*making conversation*) Carol has made up a bed for you, Isobel.

Isobel (*getting up, sniffing a little; self-consciously*) Oh. Right. I — I'll just go and get my things out of the car, then.

Isobel hastens out into the garden for a second time, grateful to be alone to gather herself

Mark and Shirley look at Gerald inquiringly. He grins sheepishly

Gerald She's a bit pissed, I'm afraid.

Mark You mustn't be taken in by tears, you know, Gerry. That's the oldest trick in the book.

Gerald Is it? Oh. I didn't know that.

Mark I think we'd better warn him, don't you, Shirl?

Gerald Warn me? What about?

Mark glances towards the garden to make sure that Isobel is not returning

Mark (*to Gerald, confidentially*) We think she's after your money.

Gerald Isobel?

Mark Yes.

Gerald Don't be daft!

Mark She said so.

Gerald What?

Mark She told us that she'd done very well out of her first three husbands, and now she was on the look-out for a fourth. That'll be you!

Gerald (*laughing*) No, no! Isobel only came to offer condolences.

Mark Well, now she'll be offering more than her condolences!

Gerald I know Isobel better than that.

Mark You don't think she drove all this way just to sample your claret, do you? You mark my words, Gerry — before you can turn around she'll be a fixture!

Gerald She won't! I've got two of those upstairs already!

Mark Well, now you've got a third.

Gerald No, I haven't! I can't imagine what Helen thought she was doing. I know she was always fond of forward planning, but she didn't need to go and fill the house with females. *I* can't cope with them on my own. *You're* going to have to give me a hand!

Mark No fear! I'm a happily-married married man. Aren't I, Shirl?

Shirley You'd better be!

Gerald I mean give me a hand to get *rid* of them! How can I live in a house with two women?

Shirley (*laughing*) Most men would give their right arm for the chance.

Mark It's not his right arm he's worried about.

Gerald (*in pathetic mode*) Now that I'm a widower — I want to be on my own. On my own with my memories of Helen. I don't want strange ladies leaving their lingerie on the bathroom radiator. (*Pointing at Mark, accusingly*) It was *you* who said that families are supposed to help you out in a crisis. Well, this *is* a bloody crisis and you're my family so you've got to get them out of here!

Shirley How can we do that if they don't want to go?

Mark Especially when they think that you don't want to be alone and they're doing you a favour.

Gerald Well, we'll have to think of *something*!

Mark Why don't you just ask them to go?

Gerald Have *you* ever tried to ask two women to do something they didn't want to do? I could never manage it with one, never mind two.

Mark But what's the problem? Just tell them that you're not *going* to be alone because you've decided to get married again. (*He smiles happily,the problem solved*)

Gerald A week after burying my wife?

Shirley Yes, Mark! What a thing to suggest!

Mark I was only trying to help.

Shirley Anyway, Daddy doesn't know anyone who would have him.

Gerald Don't you be too sure!

Mark I bet Isobel would volunteer.

Gerald Isobel's just an old friend.

Mark An old friend on the look-out for a new husband!

Gerald It's all very well for you to joke about it. *I'm* the one with a houseful of uninvited women!

Shirley Yes, Mark. We must try to be helpful.

Mark Must we?

Shirley Of course! (*She turns to her father, decisively*) It's all right, Daddy. Leave it to us! *We'll* think of something!

Gerald Oh, good! That's a great relief. Amanda's already put her house on the market, so soon there'll be no going back. (*Facing them, hopefully*) Right, then! Let's have your ideas!

Gerald waits, anticipating a flood of suggestions, but only receives a blank silence, his family failing to find any immediate inspiration

(*Impatiently*) Come on, then!

Mark Well ... er ... what sort of thing did you have in mind, Gerry?

Gerald *I* don't know, do I? That's the trouble! (*To Shirley*) I thought you two were going to help me.

Shirley We *are*, Daddy! (*To Mark*) Aren't we? (*She glares at him*)

Mark Yes! (*Then losing heart*) But ... can't you give us a rough idea?

Gerald Well, we need to find a way to make them *want* to leave.

Mark Want to leave?

Gerald Of their own accord. Something that would ... drive them out of the house!

Mark (*impressed*) Drive them out of the house, eh? I see. Right. (*A beat. Then he turns to Shirley, uncertainly*) How can we drive them out of the house, Shirl?

Shirley Tell them there are rats in the basement! (*She smiles triumphantly*)

Mark (*enthusiastically*) Good idea!

Gerald We haven't got a basement.

Mark Ah …

Shirley Squirrels in the attic?

Mark Oh, *yes*! I like it!

Shirley *We* had them once and I was terrified.

Gerald Can you imagine Amanda being frightened away by a squirrel?

Shirley No. I suppose not …

Mark No. Daft idea, Shirl.

Shirley *You* think of something, then!

Mark Yes. Right. (*He thinks hard for a moment, then grins broadly, pleased by his sudden inspiration*) Ah …!

Gerald (*delighted*) You've thought of something!

Mark Yes. I think I've got a *great* idea … !

Shirley I hope it's better than your last one!

Mark Yes — it certainly is! (*He chuckles again*)

Gerald Come on, then! Tell us!

Mark Well, what I thought was … (*He glances at Shirley and thinks better of it*) No! No, I don't think I can say it! Not in front of Shirl.

Shirley Why not?

Mark You might not approve. You might think it's a bit … (*He dismisses the idea*) No! It's not a good idea after all.

Gerald It's the only one we've got! Surely it's better than squirrels?

Mark All right. Well, what I … No — no, I couldn't suggest it! Not with Shirl listening.

Gerald (*impatiently*) Well, whisper it to me, then!

Mark hesitates, then leans across and whispers for a moment in Gerald's ear. Shirley waits, wondering. Gerald's face is a picture as he listens. When Mark has finished, Gerald laughs for a moment, then stops laughing

No! I couldn't do it!

Mark Why not?

Gerald They'd never believe me.

Mark They might.

Gerald Would *you?*

Mark No. But it's not me who's coming to live with you, is it?

Shirley Would you please let *me* into the secret?
Gerald No! No — I'm not going to do it! It's a bad idea.
Mark Can you think of a better one?
Gerald (*after a brief hesitation*) No …
Mark You've got no choice, then, have you?
Gerald No. (*He makes a firm decision*) All right — I'll do it!

Isobel returns from the garden with her overnight bag, which she raises aloft with a big smile

Isobel You see, Gerry? I've only brought an overnight bag with me, so you didn't have to worry.
Gerald I — I wasn't!
Isobel I bet you were!
Mark (*indicating her bag*) You weren't *expecting* to go home tonight, then, Isobel?
Isobel Sorry?
Mark Or do you always take an overnight bag when you travel short distance?
Isobel Well, I always think it's best to be prepared, don't you?
Mark Yes. You never know when aged widowers are going to drag you in and give you gin.

Amanda and Carol return from upstairs, obviously still in some disagreement

Amanda Gerry, I have told Mrs Capstick that there is no need for both of us to move in with you but she continues to insist.
Carol It was what Helen wanted me to do, and I'm not going back on my word!
Isobel (*to Shirley*) Your father *is* in demand, isn't he?
Shirley I think he'd prefer to live on his own.
Amanda Don't be silly, Shirley.
Carol He'd be lonely on his own.
Gerald No, he wouldn't!
Amanda (*to Gerald*) Yes, he would! You couldn't possibly cope on your own. Gerry, you were supposed to be sorting out the situation.
Gerald Was I?
Mark You don't have to worry, Aunt Amanda. (*He smiles confidently*) Gerry's got the situation under control.
Gerald (*losing heart a little*) Have I?
Mark Of course you have!
Amanda I'm relieved to hear it. Then perhaps he would inform Mrs Capstick of his decision.

Mark And not only Mrs Capstick, eh, Gerry? (*He grins at Gerald*) Off you go, then!

Gerald remains silent, uncertain how to start, so Mark tries to pave the way and turns to the ladies

You see, the thing is — Gerry's not *going* to be alone. Are you, Gerry?

Gerald Aren't I?

Mark (*impatiently*) Of course you're not!

Amanda No. He's not going to be alone because *I* shall be here.

Carol So shall I!

Amanda It does not require two women to look after one man.

Carol Well, if it has to be one it'll have to be me! I'm far more suitable.

Amanda Suitable for what, may I ask?

Carol To provide cleaning and companionship. And no strings attached!

Amanda I am not "strings", Mrs Capstick. This is a family matter, not a frivolous one. And *I* am family!

Mark (*whispering; urgently*) Come on, Gerry! What are you waiting for? Tell them!

Carol What Gerry needs is something permanent.

Amanda I *am* permanent!

Isobel (*quietly*) Yes. Like the Rock of Gibraltar.

Amanda I shall be staying with Gerry, as requested by his late wife, and that is the end of the matter.

Isobel But, Amanda, I thought you said you weren't interested in the opposite sex. You were priding yourself on your lifetime of sexual neutrality.

Amanda Gerry is not the opposite sex!

Gerald (*to Mark, aside*) Aren't I?

Mark Apparently not …

Amanda *Our* relationship will be built on friendship, not desire. Friendship and mutual respect.

Gerald (*to Mark, quietly*) That *is* a relief … !

Isobel But won't it be rather difficult for you to sustain your emotional neutrality if you're living under the same roof as Gerry? After all, he is still a very attractive man.

Gerald Thank you, Isobel. That's a much-needed boost to my morale.

Mark (*quietly*) Don't encourage her … !

Isobel So you might find that temptation got the better of you.

Amanda Gerry is not temptation.

Gerald Aren't I?

Amanda Not to me, Gerry. You're my brother-in-law.

Gerald (*to Mark, quietly*) Not the opposite sex and not temptation. I'll soon be running out of options.

Carol The last thing Gerry wants now is a lot of changes to his lifestyle.

Amanda I think *I'm* in a better position to know what Gerry wants!

Mark (*to Gerald, whispering urgently*) If you don't tell them now it'll be too late!

Gerald (*whispering*) I don't think I *can* … !

Mark (*whispering*) You must … !

Amanda He doesn't want a lot of different people to-ing and fro-ing! I have unpacked my suitcases and I'm here to stay.

Carol So am I!

Isobel (*to Shirley, with a smile*) Well, while Gerry's sorting out the problem of his ladies perhaps you'd like to show me where I'll be sleeping?

Shirley Oh — well — er — — (*She looks anxiously at Mark*)

Mark You can't do that now!

Isobel I want to unpack my bag. (*She holds up her overnight bag*)

Mark That won't take long! It's a very small bag.

Isobel And I need to spend a penny.

Mark Well, it'll have to wait!

Isobel It can't!

Mark But Gerry's got something to say!

Isobel Well, whatever he's got to say it doesn't concern *me*, does it? Come along, Shirley! Don't look so worried, Mark. We're not going for ever. (*To Amanda*) I hope you haven't taken the best bedroom, Amanda.

Isobel smiles sweetly at Amanda and goes into the hall

Shirley shrugs helplessly at Mark and follows Isobel out, closing the door behind her

Amanda I hope Isobel has no intention of overstaying her welcome …

Mark (*to Gerald, quietly*) You'd better tell them *now* — before they *all* disappear!

Amanda Yes, Gerry. The sooner you clear up the misunderstanding the better, then Mrs Capstick can return to her mother where she belongs.

Mark smiles encouragingly at Gerald, then turns importantly to the others

Mark Gerry's got something important to tell you both.

Amanda We know that, Mark. And the sooner he tells us the sooner this whole unfortunate affair can be resolved.

Mark (*chuckling hopefully*) Yes, that's what *we're* hoping, isn't it, Gerry? (*He indicates to Gerald to address the ladies*) Right — off you go!

Gerald Yes. Right. (*He turns to the ladies*) Er — er … Perhaps you'd better sit down.

Amanda There's no point in Carol sitting down when she'll soon be leaving.
Gerald Well — actually — it's not just about Carol.
Mark No — quite! (*He laughs, then stops, realizing that laughter is inappropriate*)
Carol And we have to be sitting down to hear what it is?
Gerald (*sombrely*) Yes. It would be advisable.

Amanda and Carol look at each other and then sit down on the sofa

Mark Right, then, Gerry! They're sitting down. (*He gestures encouragingly*)
Gerald Yes. Right. Now — the thing is — if you're both *really* intending to stay here — —
Amanda } (*together*) Which I am!
Carol }

Amanda and Carol both react and glare at each other

Gerald There's something you ought to know. Something which — for all *I* know — might affect your decision to remain here.
Amanda You're making it sound very mysterious.
Gerald Well ... it *is* — in a way.
Carol Mysterious?
Gerald Yes. (*He pauses uncertainly for a moment*)
Mark (*trying to encourage him*) Perhaps you'd better tell them what it is, then, Gerry!
Gerald Ah. Yes. Right. Well, you see, the thing is — and this may come as a bit of a shock to you both ... (*He hesitates again*)
Mark (*urging him on*) Yes?
Gerald The thing is — that Helen — is still here.

Amanda and Carol consider this for a moment

Amanda You said the funeral was *last* week.
Gerald Yes, it was. I didn't mean that.
Amanda But you said that Helen was still here.
Gerald Ah. I didn't mean that *Helen* was here. Helen has gone. But now she's back.

Amanda and Carol look at each other

(*To Mark, aside*) It's no good. I can't do it — !
Mark (*to Gerald, aside*) You're doing very well!
Amanda Gone but back?
Gerald Yes.

Amanda Back *here?*

Gerald Yes.

Amanda I think you'd better explain, Gerry.

Carol Yes. If Helen has gone how can she still be here?

Amanda (*an appalling thought*) The cemetery wasn't full, was it?

Gerald No, no! Nothing like that.

Amanda Then how can she still be here?

Gerald Well, she's not here — in person. But she *is* still with us.

Carol Still with us?

Gerald Yes.

Amanda Surely the undertaker didn't leave her behind?

Gerald No. No, not that.

Amanda So how can she still be with us?

Gerald Well, she's not with us — in the flesh. She's with us — in spirit.

Carol In spirit?! You don't mean — — ?

Mark Yes, he does!

Carol You mean she's come back — as a — as a ...?

Gerald Ghost. Yes. I'm afraid so.

Carol (*loudly*) She's come back as a *ghost?*

Gerald Yes. I did ask her not to.

Mark (*surprised*) Did you?

Gerald Yes.

Amanda When was this?

Gerald Oh — ages ago. It was a rainy day and we were having one of those rainy day conversations. You know the sort. And I said to Helen, "If you should happen to pre-decease me, will you promise me that you won't come back as a — er — a ... "

Mark Ghost.

Gerald Yes. But obviously she ignored my wishes.

Carol (*horrified*) You mean this house is *haunted?*

Gerald It is *now*, yes.

Amanda It never was before!

Mark Well, of course it wasn't! Nobody who had lived here had died before, had they?

Amanda Don't be ridiculous, Gerry! How can you possibly think that the house is haunted by Helen?

Gerald Well, I ... er ... (*He hesitates, uncertain of the next move*)

Mark Because she was here last night!

Gerald (*surprised*) *Was* she?

Mark (*nodding; encouragingly*) You know very well she was!

Gerald Ah — yes! (*To the ladies*) Yes. She was here last night.

Amanda You mean you *saw* her?

Gerald looks at Mark for guidance. Mark nods. Gerald turns back to the ladies

Gerald Yes. I saw her.
Carol (*intrigued*) What did she look like?
Mark She looked like Helen, of course! What do you expect her to look like? Groucho Marx?
Carol I mean — was she ... sort of ... like a white cloud? Drifting? (*She demonstrates drifting*)
Gerald Drifting?
Carol Yes. That's what they do, isn't it? (*She again demonstrates drifting*)

Gerald considers Carol's mime

Gerald Oh. No. No, I don't think she was doing anything like that. Not drifting exactly.
Mark Yes, she was!
Gerald Was she?
Mark Yes!
Gerald Oh. Right. (*To Carol*) Yes, she was. Drifting.
Amanda So *you* saw her as well, then, Mark?

Mark considers his position

Mark Er — not last night, no.
Gerald *No?*
Mark No. I ... I think it was Tuesday when *I* saw her.
Carol And was she drifting *then?*
Mark Oh, yes. Drifting quite a lot, actually.

Mark and Gerald exchange looks

Amanda And you recognized her? Even though she was ... drifting? (*She emulates Carol's mime*)
Mark Yes, certainly!
Amanda Are you seriously trying to tell us that Helen has come back to haunt us all?
Gerald Well — to haunt *me*.
Mark And me!
Gerald Yes. (*To Amanda*) Whether she intends to haunt *you* I don't know.
Mark (*to Gerald, quietly*) Of course she does! That's the whole point!

Gerald Ah. Yes. (*To Amanda*) Of course she does.

Mark She might even start throwing things.

Gerald
Carol } (*together*) Throwing things?

Mark Well, isn't that what ghosts do?

Amanda Helen never threw things when she was alive.

Mark But she's not alive now, is she? So now she might be throwing things!

Gerald I thought it was poltergeists who threw things, not ghosts …

Mark (*trying to be patient*) Gerry — a poltergeist *is* a ghost! An angry ghost!

Carol But why should Helen be angry?

Mark Because she won't be expecting to find the house full of women! Will she, Gerry?

Gerald No! She certainly won't!

Carol But it was her idea. It was Helen who asked us to move in with Gerry.

Amanda (*glaring at Carol*) Helen meant *one* of us, not *two* of us!

Gerald Ah — yes — exactly! So she won't be expecting to see *both* of you!

Mark *And* Isobel hanging about! That makes three! It'd be enough to make *anyone* throw things.

Amanda Gerry, this is quite impossible! How could Helen have come back as a ghost? She's only been buried a week.

Gerald I didn't know there was a time limit before you can make your comeback.

Carol (*sadly*) She can't have settled in yet. Surely these things take time?

Amanda Of course! You can't go one week and come back the next.

Gerald How do *we* know what the rules are? We've never been there, have we?

Mark No. For all *we* know you may be able to turn around and come straight back the minute you get there.

Carol (*thinking deeply*) Anyway, I thought that when you died — and went up there — I thought there were going to be questions and things. Isn't that what's supposed to happen?

Gerald (*on the back foot*) Ah — yes — probably. We hadn't thought of that …

Mark (*coming to the rescue*) But there wouldn't be a lot of questions for *Helen*, would there?

Gerald No? No, probably not!

Mark They'd pass her through quite quickly, I imagine.

Gerald Yes! (*Without thinking*) After all, what's three months out of a lifetime?

Mark Three months?

Gerald Oh — nothing … ! Never mind.

Mark looks puzzled

Carol If Helen's going to start throwing things perhaps you could get the vicar to exorcize her?

Gerald Oh, I don't think he'd be too keen on that. Not so soon after doing the funeral.

Amanda Gerry, I hope you don't expect us to believe all this nonsense.

Gerald (*with a shrug*) That's up to you. I just thought you ought to be informed.

Mark Yes. In case you heard ... unusual sounds in the night.

Carol (*alarmed*) Why? Was she ... wailing?

Mark looks at Carol blankly for a moment

Mark Wailing?

Carol Isn't that what ghosts are supposed to do? You know (*she demonstrates a suitably ghostly wail*) — Woo! Woo! Woo!

Gerald and Mark exchange a look, undecided about wailing

Mark Sorry?

Carol (*repeating the wail*) Woo! Woo! Woo!

The men exchange another look as they consider

Gerald No. I don't think it was anything like that. Do you, Mark?

Mark No. It was more like someone talking.

Carol You mean you had a conversation with her?

Gerald Yes, of course.

Carol (*intrigued*) What about?

A moment's silence. Gerald has not prepared this far

Mark (*anxiously*) What about, Gerry?

Gerald Ah — yes. Well, it ... it was a bit embarrassing, really.

Amanda For you or for her?

Gerald Oh, for *me!* You see ... er ... No, I can't tell you!

Amanda You must!

Gerald (*to Mark*) Must I?

Mark Yes! (*Hiding a smile*) I think you should.

Gerald (*with difficulty*) Ah. Right. Well, you see ... I was in the bathroom at the time.

Amanda In the bathroom?

Gerald Yes. Having a bath.

Amanda In the evening?

Gerald I often have a bath in the evening.

Amanda Why not in the morning?

Gerald I do that as well, sometimes.

Amanda Two baths in one day?

Mark Very clean people round here.

Carol And you heard a voice?

Gerald Yes.

Carol In the bathroom?

Gerald No. The voice was outside the bathroom.

Amanda What made you think it was Helen?

Gerald Because she called out to me.

Mark (*smiling; intrigued*) Really? Whatever did she say?

Gerald Well — this is a bit difficult for me …

Amanda It can't have been very easy for Helen — turning up and finding her widowed husband languishing in the bath!

Mark Come on, then, Gerry! What did she say?

Gerald Well, she … she called out. Because the door was shut, you see.

Amanda Surely it doesn't matter to a ghost whether a door is shut or open. Don't they just … glide through?

Gerald (*irritably*) She wouldn't just glide through, would she? Not without knocking. I was in the bath.

Carol Whatever did she say, then, Gerry?

Gerald Well, she … she called out. Quite loudly, as a matter of fact. She called out — and you're going to find this very difficult to believe — she called out, "*You're* going to be there on the Day of Judgement!"

Amanda What did she mean by that?

Gerald I think it was a reference to the amount of time I was spending in the bathroom.

Carol And you knew at once that it was Helen?

Gerald Oh, yes. You see, she always said that to me when she was alive.

Amanda "*You're* going to be there on the Day of Judgement"?

Gerald Yes. I always spent a lot of time in the bath, you see. Even when she was alive. I did query the remark, of course. I called out to her that it wasn't the Day of Judgement *yet*, and she replied that it was for *her*.

Mark has the greatest difficulty in keeping a straight face. Now running out of creative input, Gerald passes the buck

  She spoke to you, too, didn't she, Mark?

Mark (*alarmed*) Did she?

Gerald Of course she did! You told me! You remember! (*He nods encouragingly*)

Mark Oh, on — on *Tuesday?* Yes. Yes, that's right. We did have a little chat.

Amanda *You* weren't in the bathroom at the time, were you?

Mark No, no, I — — !
Amanda I thought perhaps she was a ghost who only spoke to people when they were lying down in the bath.
Mark Oh, no. No, I was in the kitchen, as a matter of fact. Standing up.
Gerald So what did she say to you?
Mark (*uncertainly*) To *me*?
Gerald In the kitchen! On Tuesday!
Mark (*thinking hard*) Ah — yes — now what *was* it … ?
Gerald Surely you remember?
Mark Do I?
Gerald Of course you do!
Mark Oh. Right. Well — er — she … she asked me to make a promise — —
Amanda *Another* promise?
Mark Yes! (*He smiles, his inspiration starting to flow*) And as *this* promise was made on *Tuesday*, after she was dead — it would obviously replace any previous promises made when she was still alive.
Gerald (*delighted by Mark's invention*) Like a codicil to a will?
Mark Yes! Exactly! (*To the others*) That's why she came back, I suppose.
Amanda To make this … codicil?
Mark Yes.
Carol What sort of promise did she ask you to make?
Mark Well … she asked me — on behalf of Shirley and myself — she asked that we — Shirley and me, that is — that we would take care of Gerry in his last few remaining years … (*He puts a fond, protective arm around Gerald; impressively*) So that's why he'll be coming to live with *us*.

Gerald thinks Mark may have over-egged the pudding and gives him a doubtful look, while Amanda and Carol digest this information

Shirley and Isobel returns from upstairs and see Gerald apparently being comforted by Mark. They wonder why

Isobel Are you all right, Gerry?

Gerald extricates himself from Mark's embrace

Gerald Yes — yes, fine. Your room OK?
Isobel Oh, yes. Very nice.
Mark Unpacked your bag all right, did you?
Isobel Yes. I think so. (*Noticing that Amanda and Carol are in a state of some uncertainty*) Is — is everything all right? You both look a little uneasy. They do look a little uneasy, don't they, Shirley?
Shirley (*looking*) Yes. They do a bit.

Amanda I'm not surprised. Gerry's been telling us all about your mother.
Shirley (*puzzled*) Sorry?
Amanda You mean he hasn't told you?
Shirley I ... I'm not sure ... (*She glances at Gerald and Mark, not sure what story they have been telling*)
Carol Gerry says that your mother has come back — as a ghost!

Gerald and Mark hold their breath, fearful that Shirley will give the game away. But she is not her father's daughter for nothing

Shirley (*calmly*) Oh, *that* — yes.

Gerald and Mark relax

Amanda (*surprised*) You mean you *know* about it?
Shirley Of course I know about it. I just didn't want *you* to know about it. Not if you're going to be staying here. It might be rather frightening in the middle of the night if you know about it.
Mark Yes! You might start thinking that you heard noises.
Isobel What *are* you talking about?
Amanda According to Gerry and Mark, Helen has come back to haunt us.

Isobel turns to look at Gerald. He shrugs, innocently

Carol Have *you* seen her as well, then, Shirl?
Shirley No, I'm afraid not, but —
Mark Yes, you have! (*He nods energetically*)
Shirley Have I?
Mark Yes!
Shirley (*compromising*) Ah — well, no, I haven't actually *seen* her — —

Gerald and Mark tense

— but I've *heard* her.

Gerald and Mark relax

Carol You *have?*
Shirley Yes. It was Tuesday, I think — —
Mark No. *I* saw her Tuesday. It must have been Thursday.
Shirley Yes, of course! That's right, darling. It was Thursday. About three in the morning. I heard this weird sound. It was going "Woo! Woo! Woo!"
Carol See! I *said* that's what they did!
Amanda But you didn't actually *see* her?

Act II   81

Shirley No. I don't think so … (*She looks at Gerald*)
Gerald Yes, you did! You saw a sort of white cloud! You remember!
Shirley A white cloud? No, I don't think so …
Gerald Yes! You did! You told me all about it! You remember!
Shirley A white cloud? No, I don't think I remember *that* …
Gerald Yes, you do! You mentioned it at breakfast! You said it was drifting.
Carol Drifting … !
Shirley (*apparently remembering*) Oh — yes — that's right! Yes. I thought it was early morning mist.
Gerald No! It was Helen!
Carol (*terrified*) Oh, dear! Perhaps I *will* only come in for two or three hours per diem … !
Amanda (*imperiously*) Pull yourself together, Mrs Capstick! Surely you don't believe them?
Carol Well, they've seen her, haven't they? And they've heard her! And they've spoken to her! I'm not staying here at night to hear wailing and see mist drifting! (*She makes for the garden door, where she turns to look back at Gerald*) Sorry, Gerry! I'll come back as usual for two or three hours per diem — but only in the daylight!

Carol departs, speedily and in fear

Amanda gets up, watching her go in surprise

Mark (*to Gerald, aside*) One down, two to go …
Amanda That girl is far too impressionable. You wouldn't have had a moment's peace if *she* was living here, Gerry. But I'm surprised at you! And you, Mark! And you, Shirley! Fancy making up a story like that. It would be quite alarming to silly, impressionable young people. (*She pauses, waiting for them to admit it*)

Gerald and Mark just look back at her, innocently

Well, it's been a long day, so if you don't mind I think I'll go up to bed now.
Gerald Yes, of course, Amanda.
Amanda Thank you for dinner, Shirley. I'm sure you did your best.
Shirley It was my pleasure.
Amanda Good-night, then, everybody!
Shirley } (*together*) Good-night!
Mark

Amanda starts to go towards the hall

Mark Don't forget to close your windows.

Amanda (*hesitating*) Sorry?
Shirley *And* lock your door ...
Amanda What do you mean?
Shirley ⎱ (*together*) Woo! Woo! Woo!
Mark   ⎰

Amanda gives them a superior smile

Amanda Don't be ridiculous!

Amanda goes, doing her best to remain immune, and closes the door behind her

They all retain their sombre mode for Isobel's sake

Mark Perhaps we'd better lock up down here, as well, eh, Shirley?
Shirley Yes, indeed! We don't want Mummy coming in *this* way, do we?

Mark and Shirley close the garden door and draw the curtains, giggling together

Isobel (*with a smile*) I didn't think ghosts needed open doors to get in, did you, Gerry?
Gerald You can never be sure!
Mark No! Better to be safe than sorry.
Shirley You wouldn't want to be woken up in the middle of the night, would you, Isobel?
Isobel Well, not by a ghost, anyway.
Mark You'll be wanting to get off *early* in the morning, I expect?
Isobel Well, not at the crack of dawn. After all, I've nothing to rush back for, have I?
Mark Haven't you? No pets? Dog? Goldfish? Something like that?
Isobel No. I'm all on my own ...
Gerald Still, you don't want to hang around here in a haunted house, do you?
Mark No, she certainly doesn't! (*To Isobel*) We'll give you a shout — oh, about seven? Then you can make an early start.
Isobel Not *too* early, I hope.
Shirley Right. We'll leave you to it, then.
Mark (*quietly*) We can't do that!
Shirley (*quietly also*) Of course we can! (*She starts to pull Mark away towards the hall*)
Gerald (*intercepting them, nervously*) Where are you off to?
Shirley We're going to bed, of course.

Gerald You don't have to go *now!*

Shirley Well, it is pretty late.

Gerald In that case we'll *all* go! (*He prepares to go*)

Isobel There's no hurry, is there, Gerry? I thought you and I were going to talk into the early hours.

Mark (*returning*) Then *I'll* stay as well!

Shirley Don't be silly, darling! Isobel hasn't seen Daddy for ages. I'm sure she's got lots of things she wants to say to him.

Mark Yes, that's what I'm worried about ... !

Shirley See you in the morning, Isobel. (*She grabs Mark's arm*) Come on, darling!

Mark But I really think we should stay and —

Shirley You're not going to let me go upstairs on my *own*, are you? (*Apparently frightened*) I might meet Mummy on the landing.

Shirley pulls Mark out into the hall, closing the door behind them

Isobel (*with a smile*) Well — your little plan seems to be working, doesn't it?

Gerald Er — sorry?

Isobel You've got rid of *one* of us already ...

Gerald I — I don't know what you mean. (*He goes to switch off the desk lamp, avoiding her eyes*)

Isobel Ghost stories at bedtime indeed! You *were* making it all up, weren't you?

Gerald (*returning to her*) No! Of course I wasn't! I — I spoke to her! So did Mark! And Shirley *heard* her!

Isobel Yes — going "Woo! Woo! Woo!" (*She laughs*)

Gerald (*losing ground*) *And* she saw mist drifting! (*He escapes to switch off the lamp on the drinks table*)

Isobel Don't worry, Gerry. I won't give you away. But I'm sure Amanda won't believe you. (*She collects her handbag and looks at him with a smile*) Mark thinks I'm after you, doesn't he? *And* after your money!

Gerald Of course he doesn't! Whatever gave you that idea?

Isobel Well, he was asking me a lot of questions.

Gerald No, no — I'm sure the idea never even entered his head!

Isobel (*going to him*) After all, you and I are just old friends, aren't we?

Gerald Yes — of course we are!

Isobel Good old friends.

Gerald Yes.

Isobel With a secret.

Gerald Yes ...

Isobel Nothing more than that.

Gerald No.

Isobel Anyway, I don't live all that far away. So you always know where you can find a good old friend. If you ever *do* need one.

Gerald (*uncertainly*) Ah. Yes. Right.

Isobel And thank you for the talk. It did help. (*She kisses him lightly on the cheek*) Good-night, Gerry.

Gerald smiles at her fondly

Gerald Good-night, Isobel.

Amanda bursts in from the hall in a bit of a state

Amanda (*calling loudly*) Isobel!

Gerald and Isobel look at her in surprise

Isobel Whatever's the matter?

Amanda I — I was on my way to the bathroom — to brush my teeth — and I — I thought I saw a — a white figure — drifting along the landing!

Gerald points at Amanda triumphantly

Gerald There you are, you see! What did I tell you? (*He laughs*)

Amanda (*hastily trying to preserve her dignity*) Of course, it *was* rather dark, and I'm sure it was only my imagination ... But, Isobel — perhaps I could share *your* room tonight?

Isobel grins at Gerald, and goes to Amanda

Isobel Yes, of course you can! (*She takes Amanda's arm*) And if you want to go home in the morning I can give you a lift.

Amanda (*a little embarrassed*) Oh, I couldn't do that. I couldn't leave Gerry all alone. I promised.

Gerald It's all right, Amanda. You don't have to worry about me. After all, I shan't *be* alone, shall I? Not now Helen's come back. (*He smiles contentedly*)

Amanda looks at him uncertainly and Isobel tries to hide her amusement

Isobel That's settled, then! I'll help you pack in the morning. Good-night, Gerry!

Isobel and Amanda go into the hall, arm in arm. As they go, Isobel looks back, winks at Gerald, and closes the door behind them

Gerald chuckles, happy and relieved. He wanders back to look fondly at the photograph of Helen

Gerald You'd never believe what's been going on here tonight! (*He smiles, and then picks up the photograph to look at Helen, sadly but rather put out*) Why did you have to go first? *I* wanted to do that … ! (*He kisses her, replaces the photograph and starts to go towards the hall*)

But before he reaches the door it suddenly swings open — as if by magic! Gerald looks at the door, deeply puzzled, and allows his imagination to run away with him

Helen … ? (*He looks uncertainly in the other direction*) Helen … ! You haven't *really* come back, have you? (*Then he dismisses the idea, his common sense reasserting itself*) No! No, of course you haven't! Must have been a gust of wind blowing the door open.

Gerald starts to go into the hall, smiling at his foolish imagination. He hesitates in the doorway and looks back, not completely certain. Then he smiles, switches the lights off and goes, leaving the door open

The room is now only lit by moonlight shining between the curtains and the light from the hall spilling in through the open door

A moment's pause after Gerald has disappeared. Then the door slowly closes itself. A light comes up on the photograph of Helen and we hear her gentle fond laughter as — —

The Lights fade slowly to Black-out

CURTAIN

FURNITURE AND PROPERTY LIST

ACT I

On stage:
Sofa
Sofa table (above) *On it*: magazine
Coffee table (R of sofa) *On it*: dish of nuts
Armchair
Desk. *On it*: lamp, family photographs
Table. *On it*: photograph of Helen
Drinks table. *On it*: whisky, brandy, sherry, gin, tonic, glasses, lamp
Television set
Bookcases
On walls: paintings, looking-glass

Off stage:
Shopping bags (full) *In one*: evening paper (**Shirley**)
Laptop computer (**Mark**)
Briefcase with documents and small package of salmon sandwiches in it (**Mark**)
Bunch of lilies (**Amanda**)
Vase with lilies (**Mark**)

Personal:
Shirley: handbag
Amanda: handbag

ACT II

On stage:
Check position of sandwiches under sofa

Off stage:
Apron (**Isobel**)
Two cups of coffee (**Mark**)
Cup of coffee (**Amanda**)
Overnight bag (**Isobel**)

LIGHTING PLOT

Practical fittings required: lamps on desk and drinks table, flicker effect from TV
One interior with hall and window backing.The same throughout

ACT I

To open: General interior and exterior lighting; early evening in late summer

| Cue 1 | **Gerald** switches on the TV | (Page 1) |
| | *Bring up flicker effect from TV* | |

| Cue 2 | **Gerald** switches off the TV | (Page 1) |
| | *Cut flicker effect* | |

| Cue 3 | As **Mark** and **Shirley** follow **Gerald** out | (Page 42) |
| | *Fade all lights to black-out* | |

ACT II

To open: Lights up on hall and kitchen backings; late summer lighting on garden backing, fading to moonlight during the act

| Cue 4 | **Gerald** switches on the drinks table lamp | (Page 44) |
| | *Switch on lamp* | |

| Cue 5 | **Mark** switches on the lights | (Page 44) |
| | *Snap on general interior lighting* | |

| Cue 6 | **Gerald** switches on desk lamp | (Page 45) |
| | *Switch on lamp* | |

| Cue 7 | **Gerald** switches off desk lamp | (Page 83) |
| | *Switch off lamp* | |

| Cue 8 | **Gerald** switches off drinks table lamp | (Page 83) |
| | *Switch off lamp* | |

| Cue 9 | **Gerald** switches main lights off | (Page 85) |
| | *Snap off general interior lighting* | |

| Cue 10 | Hall door closes itself | (Page 85) |
| | *Bring up spot on photogaph of Helen* | |

| Cue 11 | **Helen**'s laughter is heard | (Page 85) |
| | *Slowly fade all lights to black-out* | |

EFFECTS PLOT

ACT I

ACT II